TEACHING STUDENTS PHYSICAL EDUCATION THROUGH A MOVEMENT EDUCATION APPROACH

TEACHING STUDENTS PHYSICAL EDUCATION THROUGH A MOVEMENT EDUCATION APPROACH

Timothy Sawicki

The Edwin Mellen Press
Lewiston, New York
www.mellenpress.com

Library of Congress Cataloging-in-Publication Data

Library of Congress Control Number: 2020952866

Sawicki, Timothy.
   Teaching students physical education through a movement education approach / Timothy Sawicki.

1. Education--Physical education. 2. Education--Research. 3. Education--Teaching methods & materials--general.
       p. cm.
   Includes bibliographical references.
   ISBN-13: 978-1-4955-0857-8 (softcover)
   ISBN-10: 1-4955-0857-9 (softcover)
   I. Title.

hors série.

The Edwin Mellen Press
Box 450
Lewiston, New York
USA 14092-0450

Printed in the United States of America

To order books, telephone 1-716-754-2788
or
go to mellenpress.com

Dedicated to Louise

Contents

Preface

There is no career more satisfying than teaching physical education. I would like to thank all the students, individuals and fellow colleagues I have met along the journey who helped to inspire this book, and those who contributed by volunteering information used within these pages.

Early in my teaching career, one of my Grade 10 students named Ronny made me realize my approach to teaching physical education, although different from the norm, was on the right track. It started when I asked the students in the class while taking attendance, "Where is Ronny?" The students replied, "He does not come to phys ed." I taught several more lessons without Ronny when, one day, I noticed him peering into the gymnasium from the doorway. The next day, I called his name as he was again watching from the doors and he ran away. But after about three weeks Ronny was sitting on the bleachers watching the class.

I soon learned students were talking about my classes outside of physical education and Ronny was listening in. After a month or so, Ronny was dressed in whites and participating in class. The other students said he had never done that before. My approach to teaching physical education was making waves. It is an approach that is all inclusive, highly-geared toward enjoyment and cooperation, and highly-opposed to sports skills learning. I use scoring

i

and winning as motivation and do not have the students on the same teams, do not have them with the same partners, and often pair the weakest with the strongest. I change how to score, where to score, and who can score (sometimes while activities or game play is taking place). Using a movement education approach allows variations in how general skills are learned which decreases boredom and increases fundamental skill acquisition. I would like to thank Ronny and all the students who accepted me and my different way of teaching physical education throughout the years.

Although I am closing in on retirement, and my journey in teaching is nearing an end, it has been enjoyable and full of self-discovery and reflection. Like the Hobbit in Lord of the Rings or Dorothy in the Wizard of Oz, there have been so many exciting adventures along the way, and all I can leave is a few final teaching ideas this book provides. This book is intended to be used for the Movement Education class at Canisius College as a supplement to teacher training content in the course, but any teacher from K-12 is welcome to use its ideas. The movement approach to teaching physical education shown in the book is a collection of all I have learned about physical education across a lifetime of wonderful experiences.

Dr. Timothy Sawicki

Chapter One

Introduction

Teaching physical education can be an exciting and rewarding career. After teaching physical education in elementary and high school, I realized I had an opportunity to influence the future of physical education in schools through working in a teacher training program. Over the years, I have developed a way of teaching physical education which is a conceptual approach encompassing the early grades and can be adapted right through to high school. While slightly unorthodox, it comes from my belief that physical education class is a place for all students to learn and enjoy physical activity no matter their natural or learned sport skill level, or lack thereof.

This book was created because I saw a need for physical education teachers to consider new ways of teaching. A need to move away from a traditional sports skills approach to teaching physical education. Studies in general have shown that over 50% of students will opt out of taking physical education when given the chance. Further, physical education teachers should realize that their students will likely never use the physical skills they have learned in class once they leave the school system. For example, I have never used the soccer chip kick, banana kick, or instep kick since leaving high school physical education where I was taught and graded on these skills. As teachers we must consider closely what we are doing and why we are doing it.

As our students move into the work world, qualities such as communication, cooperation, and teamwork are critical to employers. Skills like the soccer chip kick, shoelace kick, and instep kick are not so useful in the work world. Therefore, we as physical education teachers should use sports skills as a means to teach life skills rather than using them as the ultimate goal of learning.

A Conceptual Approach

Physical education can be viewed as an academic (school) discipline, but unfortunately it lacks a conceptual approach to teaching. There is no developmental stage approach to teaching physical education as all the other academic school subjects have. For example, math has the developmental approach of teaching addition and subtraction first, followed by division and multiplication, long-division, fractions, then on to teaching ratios, etc. As the grade levels progress, there are clearly defined mathematical concepts that must be taught and learned before the student can move on. English takes a similar approach. Students are taught reading and printing first, followed by writing and the use of nouns, verbs and adjectives, etc.

Physical education, however, has not developed a similar movement-based conceptual approach to skill learning. For example, you may see dribbling with a soccer ball done in first grade as a lesson focus, and you will likely also see this done in third grade and fifth grade and seventh grade and ninth grade and on through the conclusion of high school. Physical educators teach the same skills over and over again through all the grade levels. In defense of physical education as a discipline, there is an abundance of skills to be learned and creating an approach to teaching each skill at a certain grade level would be an arduous task. Therefore, a movement-based conceptual approach to teaching physical education is a difficult task but one that needs to be considered.

One suggested approach to teaching physical education is through the progressive development of skills changing through each grade level along with expanding the goals of each lesson to include life skills. Teaching strictly sport-specific skills as the basis of the curriculum year after year is not recommended. What is recommended is dividing the year-long curriculum into distinct parts and teaching skills that are developmentally appropriate. For example, students in kindergarten to grade three (K-Gr.3) would work on sending, receiving, and maintaining lessons throughout the year. These skills are learned in the broadest sense along with other goals from the social, emotional, and cognitive domains such as teamwork (social), safety (cognitive), etc. The physical education teacher should use many different balls, equipment, and objects during the year-long curriculum. The activities should be low organizationally and simple for the children to master. During the early years of physical education, teachers should avoid the introduction of sports-specific skills that the children are not yet motorically ready for.

In the next stage in elementary school teaching (Gr.4-Middle School), the focus shifts to fundamental skill learning, with special day activities (discussed later) sporadically placed throughout the year. Fundamental skills are general skills that lead up to learning sports-specific skills. These include running, jumping, hopping, skipping etc. Unfortunately, physical educators have not always taken the best approach to developing the fundamental skills in elementary school children. Research has shown physical educators rush through development of fundamental skills or skip them altogether in favor of playing games. Further, the students in the class will often eagerly press the teacher to play a game instead of the "boring" skill lessons. The problem with this is that many of the students have not yet learned the fundamental skills necessary to play these games properly, so progressing through the drills too quickly to get to the game is not wise for the good of the students.

Elementary school physical education teachers (Gr.4-Middle School) should break the curriculum up into fundamental skills and teach them week by week. It is best to start with loco-motor skills such as running, skipping, and hopping and progress to the more difficult skills such as kicking and striking at the end of the curriculum. Through the use of movement education themes (discussed later), I recommend teaching loco-motor skills first. The loco-motor skills taught can be running, sliding, hopping, skipping, galloping, leaping and jumping. These fundamental skills can be taught singly as a lesson focus or combined together, i.e., lesson focus on skipping and hopping. After the loco-motor skills have been practiced the teacher can progress to the manipulative fundamental skills such as throwing, catching, hand dribble, foot dribble, striking, and kicking. Each of these manipulative fundamental skills can be taught alone or combined with each other or with loco-motor skills, i.e., running and throwing. It is suggested that skills are not combined until later in elementary school with the curriculum in the early elementary grades divided into single fundamental skill lessons.

During the middle school years, more traditional sports-specific skill learning can begin. I call these sports-related skills. For example, the curriculum can be divided into basketball skills, soccer skills, lacrosse skills, etc. This in no way implies the teacher should play the traditional sport during this curriculum. It only means the students are developmentally ready to begin traditional sports-skills learning. Middle school is a time when sports-specific learning can take place if the fundamental skills have been previously learned. The middle school years are a good time to use modified sports-specific activities and games (Sawicki, 2000) that are not the traditional version of the game. For example, playing baseball by striking with a tennis racquet or hitting a tennis ball off a t-ball stand.

At the high school stage, the teacher can divide the curriculum into sports-specific learning. Traditional activities such as soccer, basketball, floor hockey, and lacrosse can be taught if the fundamental skills have been learned in elementary school, along with appropriate lead-up skills during the middle school years.

The conceptual approach I have presented here is a progressive developmental model of teaching physical education much like mathematics, science and English have done for years. Using the conceptual approach to physical education, the teacher starts by doing low organizational activities in the early years (K-Gr.3) which focus on very general skills learning, then the elementary stage focuses on fundamental skills learning (Gr.4 to Middle School), middle school teaches sports-related activities without playing traditional games, and the high school years focus on traditional sports skills. Too often, physical education teachers introduce specific sports skills too early in their physical education curriculum, creating a detrimental snowball effect resulting in students being ill-prepared for the next stage of learning.

Special day activities are one (or more) day unique activities interspersed throughout the elementary, middle, and high school curriculum. These activities are not necessarily skill development activities but develop physical skills like balance, strength, and flexibility secondarily and can improve the body's movement capabilities. The special day activities tend to focus on the other domains such as affective, social or cognitive domains. Special day activities could be (but are not limited to) swimming, gymnastics, dance, archery, biking, roller-blading, adventure activities, orienteering, parachute activities, fitness, ice-skating, and weight training lessons. An example of an elementary curriculum including special day activities may be, after two weeks of loco-motor lessons on running, the teacher incorporates a special day activity parachute lesson.

Special Day Activity- Parachute Lesson

Through the use of a conceptual movement education approach to teaching physical education, more children will experience success in physical education and therefore be more likely to continue engaging in physical activity throughout their schooling and lifetime. Further, learning sports skills should not be the ultimate goal of physical education. Instead, teaching developmentally-appropriate skills combined with life skills should be the goal.

Success in Physical Education Classes

Using a conceptual approach to teaching physical education allows children to develop skills in a progressive developmental way and allows them to experience success while learning. Teaching developmentally-appropriate skills during the elementary years through a movement education approach allows children to gain success and confidence in the activities that will turn them on to physical education. Research has shown that roughly 70% of children opt out of physical education and community sports during the high school years (Sawicki, 2000). Based on that statistic it must be concluded that physical educators are not turning children on to physical activity and that a lack of experiencing success early on would be a major reason for them opting out. Allowing children to experience success by learning the skills that are developmentally-appropriate at an early age will help them develop a positive attitude towards physical education. All too often, teachers allow students to play games that only the naturally gifted athletic students will excel at. This creates a large discrepancy between the few gifted athletes and the many students who needed further skill development. By allowing students to experience

7

success early on in physical education classes using the movement education approach, teachers can turn all students on to physical activity.

Local Public school students join in at the Canisius College Gymnasium

Although developmentally-appropriate skill learning is a focus of all physical education lessons it should be viewed as only one part of a physical education curriculum. Learning skills is the vehicle in which we experience success and develop a life-long positive attitude towards physical activity. So why do physical educators teach sports-specific skills so religiously to their students? It was stated earlier in this book that the chances of students ever using any of the sports skills we teach them when they become adults is remote. Why then are physical educators requiring these skills so adamantly?

There are a few reasons why physical educators opt for a sports skills model. The first is that it is easy to plan and teach a lesson using sports skills. It takes a great deal more planning and preparation to teach lessons that are both developmentally-appropriate and accomplish goals from more than one domain (physical, social, cognitive, affective). The second is that traditions in the school have always been toward a sports skills approach. A final and self-serving reason is so that physical education can allow the athletes from the school's sports teams more practice time. It should be noted that the good for the majority of students is sacrificed when physical education is used as a practice venue for school athletes.

Learning of skills should be viewed as a way for children to gain an array of abilities and experience success so they will develop a positive outlook on physical activities. Essentially, most students will never use any of the physical skills they learned in physical education. The number one hiring criteria of CEOs of major corporations is employees who can communicate and work well with others. Performing a technically correct banana kick would not be on that criteria list. Physical educators need to take a close look at the curriculum they teach their students and ensure the focus is on using skills as a means to teach various life skills the students will need when they leave school.

Movement Education Themes

Movement education is a school physical education approach which uses movement themes to provide variety to the skills learning during a lesson. Movement education also allows for student success and provides a wide array of

9

learning goals beyond skills. Themes are a useful lesson plan tool to add fun and variety to the lesson. Using a movement education theme combined with a fundamental skill ensures the students will enjoy the lesson.

All physical lesson plans should include four things: a developmentally appropriate skill(s), a theme, a sub-theme, and an outcome(s)/goal(s) which are physical and/or social, affective, or cognitive.

A theme is a major area of concentration used to make the skill learning variable. Movement themes are: Body Awareness, Space Awareness, Effort Qualities, and Relationships. A sub-theme must be selected along with a theme in every lesson, and the chosen theme and sub-theme should be used throughout the entire lesson.

The movement education themes and sub-themes below can be applied to age-appropriate skills that are learned.

Theme: Body Awareness - How the body moves.

Sub-Theme

1. Functions (stretch, bend, twist, curl)

2. Body parts

3. Transfer of weight focus

Theme: Space Awareness - Where the body or object can move throughout space.

Sub-Theme

1. Directions (forward, backwards, sideways)

2. Pathways (curved, zig-zag, straight)

3. Levels (high, medium, low)

Theme: Effort Qualities – The speed of the object or body moving through space.

Sub-Theme

1. Speed/time (fast, slow)

2. Weight (fine, firm)

Theme: Relationships - Working with an object or person or group of people.

Sub-Theme

1. To an object

2. To a partner

3. To a small group (3-4)

4. To a large group

A lesson plan for elementary age teaching (Gr.4- Middle School) would include a fundamental skill such as throwing and a movement theme and sub-theme such as Space Awareness - high and low. Envisioning some of the activities (in short form) of the lesson: throw to the wall high, throw to the wall low, throw to a partner high, throw to a partner low, etc. The use of a theme and sub-theme allows the teacher to plan a lesson in which the highlighted skill is performed in a variety of learning ways. By having variety in the lesson students are thought to become more skillful movers because they have learned to be more flexible and more adaptable when performing a skill. The principle of variability of practice and schema theory has support in skill learning literature from the field of motor learning skill acquisition (Schmidt, Lee, Winstein, Wulf and Zelanik,

2018). It can therefore be concluded that movement education having students practicing skills in many different ways leads to better skilled players. By becoming better skilled, students will experience success. They will be turned on to physical education and be more likely to take away from the experience a positive outlook on physical activity. With a positive attitude towards physical activity, a life-long desire to participate in activity is more likely.

The use of themes and sub-themes evolved out of the work of Rudolph Laban in the 1950s in England and Europe. For years, physical education used a lot of calisthenics for the content of the lessons and was very militaristic. The reason for this regimented style of physical education was so the classes could train the students in case they were needed to go to war. Schools during the 1950s were thinking of the possibility of war just as it had in the 1940s. Students needed to be kept fit and ready for action. Laban saw a need for a more flexible way to teach physical education and he offered community dance and gymnastics classes using a movement education approach. The movement education approach which evolved out of Laban's work is a freer and more open way of learning skills. Laban's approach created controversy but opened the door for the teachers who studied under him to begin teaching physical education away from calisthenics and military drills. It was still regimented in some ways (students wore white t-shirts, white shorts and no shoes) but allowed for flexibility in the way it was taught and the way skills were learned.

From this early beginning in the 1950s in Europe, physical education has evolved into a much more student-centered approach that allows for exploration and flexibility in teaching skills. Students should be given a wide variety of tasks to learn through practicing them in a variety of ways. This leads to more skillful movers. Movement education is the best approach for teaching physical education at all ages.

Lesson Planning

Lessons in physical education should be composed of several parts. The sections may differ slightly from teacher to teacher but will generally stay the same across the curriculum. Planning a lesson begins with a skill selection. If the children are younger (K-Gr.3) then maintaining, receiving, or sending lesson plans are developed. If the students are at an elementary age (Gr.4-Middle School) then a fundamental skill(s) is chosen. If the students are late middle school or early high school aged, then sport-related skills are chosen. If the students are in later high school, then sports-specific skills are used as the lesson content.

After the selection of the skill, a theme and sub-theme(s) are chosen. This gives the lesson variety. To this point, the lesson has a skill(s) and theme and sub-theme, i.e., **Skill:** Throwing, **Theme:** Effort Qualities, **Sub-Theme:** Fine and Firm (Light/Hard).

Following the Skill, Theme and Sub-theme, other information is added such as Outcomes (Goals) of the lesson (social, affective/emotional, physical and cognitive), Teaching Tips, Equipment needed, and any other information that may help the teacher with the lesson presentation. This information is written at the top of the lesson plan and is called the introductory section. Under a teaching tips section, the teacher may want to include a safety aspect of the lesson. It is wise to discuss safety in each lesson as this will provide legal documentation that the teacher is concerned with safety in every lesson he/she teaches.

The next three sections of the lesson plan are the lesson activities. The lesson begins with a **Warm Up**. In a 50-minute lesson the warm up should be short (i.e., 5 minutes). The warm up allows the muscles too be heated and a stretching routine might be included after some movement has taken place. The stretching is used to decrease the chance of injury caused by strain on the muscles. Teachers should avoid having the students jog around the gymnasium using the same pattern each day (i.e., jog around the perimeter of the gymnasium in a square pattern). This becomes monotonous for the students and warm ups become boring. Creating fun and invigorating warm ups each day is one of the most challenging parts of planning a lesson.

Local Public school students join in at the Canisius College Gymnasium

The second section of the lesson is the **Skill Development** section. This is the most important section of the lesson but tends to be the least considered and planned for part. The students need to develop the skills of the lesson and so this section is imperative for students. The skill development section should take between 20-30 minutes in a 50-minute lesson. It resembles a series of drills that is commonly seen in coaching practices. As mentioned earlier, one common problem for the teacher is when students eagerly suggest the class get to the game and skip the skill development activities. The teacher should reinforce to the students that they can only play the game after they've mastered the skills necessary to do so.

The last section of the lesson is the **Culminating Activity/Game**. This section should not be viewed as the most important part of every lesson but instead be used as a reward and challenge for the class after learning the skill(s) of the day. The culminating activity usually takes 15-20 minutes (of 50-minute lesson). Awards are a great idea to encourage good class participation. Having a variety of awards to hand out throughout the year ensures all students at one time or another will receive one for being on the winning team. Awards can be paper generated and simply created by the teacher (see https://www.creativecertificates. com/physical-education-certificates/).

In summary, lesson plans begin with a warm up that gets the muscles in the body heated and can be paired with a brief stretching session. Most warm up activities incorporate running but the teacher may also want to incorporate the skill focus into the warm up. For example, if throwing is the fundamental skill focus of the day, then the warm up may include throwing.

It has been established that teaching fundamental skills is imperative for elementary physical education teachers and that the use of movement education themes will provide the necessary variety for a positive learning experience. The body of the lesson (skill development) comes after the warm up and should take up most of the lesson time. This time is spent on learning the skill of the day. In a 50-minute lesson the teacher could have the students work on skills for 20-30 minutes or more but leave some time for a fun game at the end. Research shows that the skill development part of the lesson is the most important part for students but is the part physical education teachers do the most inadequate job with. Often the teachers will skip through skill development too quickly or move right to the game which students are not developmentally ready for.

The lesson concludes with a Culminating Activity/ Game that has the lesson skill focus as its main objective. For a teacher to decide what game is appropriate, he/she needs to determine how the points of the game are scored and what skill is used to score them. For example, a football-like game would be most appropriate for a lesson where the skill focus is catching because in order to score points in football you need to catch a football. A game like basketball (shooting into a target) has throwing as the skill focus to score points. The game the teacher decides to use should evolve naturally out of the lesson skill focus.

One of the exciting parts of a physical education class is the culminating activity/game. Research shows that 70% of physical education lessons have games as their focus.

Physical education teachers must be careful not to have games as a focus by omitting developmental skills learning, but games are a fun and integral part of physical education lessons. Games also allow skills to be tested in a moving and ever changing environment where pressure is added in a fun way. Many traditional games must be carefully considered. Traditional games such as dodge ball, musical chairs, duck-duck goose are not only counter-productive to skill development but actually have many negative consequences. Physical education teachers and even state agencies have gone so far as to ban games like dodge ball because of these negative consequences. (Williams, 1992).

Another consideration of lesson planning is lesson progression. The teacher should ensure the skill practice progresses from small group, i.e., one person to partners to small group activities. Individual work to partner work to three person or larger group activities will create lesson flow and progression. Further, having the activities progress from stationary to moving will also help the flow of the lesson. A last consideration when teaching using lesson progression is to start with simple activities and move to more complex activities.

Qualities of a Good Lesson/Good Teaching

There is an abundance of qualities that make up good lesson and teaching qualities. The expectation is that practicing student teachers will learn the essential ingredients of a good lesson and good teaching. As a student progresses through physical education upper years, where teaching methods classes are taken, more and more items are added to a checklist of required lesson qualities and teacher behaviors. There is a continuum in teacher evaluations which culminates in an evaluation during student teaching which may include be up to 30 qualities. The five main qualities of a good lesson/teacher (which are each divided into many sub-qualities) that should be learned and understood for movement educators are: achievement of the skill and theme, maximum participation, professional attitude, personal enthusiasm and supervisory duties/safety.

Achievement of the Skill and Theme

The teacher begins planning a lesson by selecting a skill (broad based, i.e., maintaining in (K-Gr.3), fundamental skills (Gr.4-Middle School), sports related skills (late Middle School), sports specific skills (High School) that is developmentally appropriate for the students. The chosen skill should be the focus of the lesson activities and be maintained throughout the entire lesson. For example, if catching (Gr.4-Middle School) is chosen as the skill of the day then catching should be a part of all activities. Further, the culminating activity at the end of the lesson should focus on have catching as the way points or goals are scored. Using an earlier example, a football type game would have a catching focus for the culminating game because to score a touchdown the player has to catch the ball. Keeping the skill focus from the start of the lesson through the activity at the end of the lesson allows for optimal practice of the activity and is the first quality of a good lesson.

Likewise, the chosen theme and sub-theme should occur through the entire lesson. If possible, the warm up should include the skill and theme and sub-theme. Introducing the theme and sub-theme in all parts of the lesson allows for variety while practicing the skill of the day. Themes decrease boredom and increase fun while learning a skill. Drills done in past physical education programs have tended to be lacking in variety and therefore the students were easily bored.

Maximum Participation

It is important that every student in the gymnasium participates (unless injured). Maximizing participation by decreasing the size of lines is a good rule of thumb for teachers to follow, i.e., smaller groups and more groups. We have all walked into a gymnasium or coaching practice and seen a line of 30 students waiting to take their turn at a skill. If someone were to count the amount of time it takes for the last player in line to get his/her first turn, it could be several minutes before he/she gets a chance to practice the skill.

Incorrect Formation – a long line of students and one net and ball

XX XXX XXX XXX XXX XXX XXX XXX XXX

<u>Correct Formation</u>- many goals and small groups of students

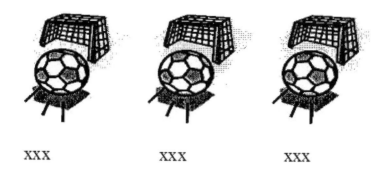

XXX   XXX   XXX

In terms of lesson planning, maximum participation should be used in all activities. If a teacher is having children shoot at a basketball hoop, use all the basketball hoops in the gymnasium. If there are only two hoops in the gymnasium, then modify the equipment by using garbage cans for shooting baskets. Having children line up in a huge line will decrease participation and practice time. If you were to count how long it takes a child standing in a line of 30 students to take two shots (one each time through the line), it may equate to five minutes or more. This translates to practicing throwing only once every few minutes. Within no time, the teacher will find the class is over and that each student has had very little practice at the skill. Teachers must consciously be aware of how much practice time is being provided. Having many groups with lots of equipment and offering as many attempts as time allows will undoubtedly improve the student's skill level. I have seen a teacher line up three students across a single basketball hoop to shoot at and this allows for maximum participation.

Although the previous example creates lots of action in shooting three basketballs at once, it drastically decreases wait times (as opposed to one student going at a time in one long line). Teachers need to be innovative and organized when preparing for maximum participation during skill development activities.

During the culminating activity (using the rule of the thumb) the teacher would make more goals than traditionally used, i.e., four goals or even six goals and have smaller groups of students on each team. This increases practice time and maximizes participation rates. If there is a time when there is an uneven number of players on a team, the teacher should have one team play with fewer players and have all players play. Sitting players out to even the numbers sets a bad precedent. It is suggested that the team with one less player be a little stronger in skill (which is carefully and craftily chosen by the teacher so the students are unaware of it). The teacher choosing teams wisely will eliminate the need to sit players out.

Professional Attitude

A professional attitude involves looking and acting the part of a seasoned physical education teacher. An important part of a professional attitude is considering professional deportment in dress. Physical education teachers should realize whatever the teacher wears present a statement to the students about what he/she personally endorses. Rather than wearing a name brand product, it is recommended the teacher wear plain clothing without logos. In this way students can also be asked to wear certain non-statement oriented clothing and disagreements about what is appropriate dress can be minimized. In essence, the teacher is being a role model for the students. Teachers should strongly consider wearing a professional looking track suit and avoid regular clothes such as casual pants. Some physical education teachers may feel it is fine to wear casual clothes (sometimes veteran teachers who unfortunately no longer concern themselves with professional deportment as much as new teachers do). It is recommended teachers closely consider what they wear and set a good example for the students and for anyone who may watch their teaching environment, i.e., principal.

Dressing appropriately is one aspect of professional attitude. Having a good rapport with students and being organized are other aspects that are qualities of a good teacher. The teacher should be organized and plan the lesson so equipment is ready to go for each activity. This may involve setting up the next lesson activity while students are still working on one. The teacher should also anticipate that students may find some activities boring and unstimulating. No matter how much planning, work and faith goes into the lesson planning, the fact is that some activities will not go as well as the teacher planned. Therefore, the teacher should plan alternate activities for each lesson or plan changes to activities on the spot. Making changes on the spot is one of the most difficult aspects of teaching and is called 'thinking on your feet.' It is a challenge for all teachers to modify the activities while the activities are taking place. Once a teacher can make on the spot changes to the activities he/she will be one step closer to being an excellent teacher.

Personal Enthusiasm

In some cases, the teacher has limited opportunities to impress students and turn them on to physical education. Making the most out of the lesson involves using your personal strengths and doing the outmost within yourself to make the lesson work. If a teacher is naturally comical then he/she can bring this aspect into their teaching (walking the fine line between developing a fun atmosphere and not being taken seriously). If the teacher is quiet and sincere then he/she can bring the class in close to talk to everyone. The teacher should use his/her strengths to work around any weaknesses. Some common characteristics that the teacher should remember are to be outgoing, professional, and to have fun when teaching. Think of teaching as you would about the hiring process or a teacher evaluation. You may have just one chance to show how good a teacher you are and you should make the most of it.

Another aspect of personal enthusiasm is to be creative. The fundamental notion about being creative is to develop activities in the lesson that students have never done before and make the activities fun. One way in which creativity can be incorporated is by having new names for the games, players, and teams involved in the activities. For example, the Blue Jays versus the Red Sox versus the Yankees etc. Creative props should also be built and used during the activities. One of the quickest ways to reduce student excitement (which is unwanted) is to play games that do not fit into the natural flow of the lesson or to do activities that the students have done many times before. It is the teacher's job to come up with his/her own ideas and new ideas that are modified and adapted from existing activities. Playing games like 'What Time is it Mr. Wolf' or 'Red Light — Green Light,' are old activities that have been done by the students, probably since kindergarten, and shows little creativity on the teacher's part. Making props, using poster boards, cutting out shapes for the floor, and creating new ways to use equipment is all part of being a good teacher. Making equipment is a cheap and creative way to aid in your teaching. Common inexpensive materials can be used and brought in by students or the students themselves can create equipment to use. Modified equipment will be shown in a later chapter of this book.

Supervisory Duties

Supervisory duties require a teacher to watch the student's behavior, look out for safety concerns, and monitor what is happening with the students in the class. The teacher should plan in advance for what happens if a student needs a drink (having a whole class scheduled drink break may take up to 10 minutes of a physical education class). Other considerations to plan in advance are what to do with students who ask to go to the washroom, what happens when the teacher forgets or needs a piece of equipment, what does the teacher do with students who are not feeling well and do not want to participate. Teachers should plan for every question possible and have a solution in advance for any questions the students may ask.

Another aspect of supervisory duties is to monitor safety and watch what students are doing. Students who do not follow safety rules should receive consequences previously set out by the teacher (called 'Classroom Rules'). This may involve time outs or re-doing the activity in the appropriate and safe way. Teachers have to work with all students in the gymnasium and students who are not listening and are not cooperating should have penalties imposed. Being aware of what is going on in the gymnasium with many students moving in different directions at once is a challenge all physical education teachers face.

Some of the more common thoughts a beginning teachers should have are planning ahead for common problems in the gymnasium like behavioral problems, washroom/water questions, how you will move from one activity to the next, how can you modify and change each activity if it is not working, whether or not the activity chosen for the age of the group is too easy or too complicated, having awards on hand to give out for good class participation or the winning team or for certain parts of the lesson, how he/she will get equipment out and manage it during the lesson, how line ups will move from place to place in the gymnasium, and how to maintain consistent participation for all students.

It is a good idea for the teacher to physically go through the lesson before going live with it in a class. At a minimum, the teacher should go through the lesson mentally to determine whether or not it will work. Teachers must watch students moving in and out of boundary areas and plan the consequences for this, practice your voice commands and what you will say and how you will make sure everyone hears you. These are common problems and struggles beginning teachers face and teachers have to plan carefully to avoid them.

One phrase I like to say to the students I am training in teachers' college is that teaching is just that, teaching. Many times beginning teachers plan a series of activities and then go through the lesson as planned and are oblivious to what is happening with the students in his/her class. This is what I refer to as monitoring a lesson instead of teaching a lesson. To properly teach a lesson, the teacher must teach the skills, correct the skills, change and manage student behavior, watch for safety concerns, and change activities when necessary. In contrast, many physical education teachers simply monitor a lesson, meaning they continue on with the planned activities whether or not they are working. The teacher will forget to watch what is happening and instead focus on getting the lesson done as it was planned.

The challenge for physical education teachers is to think on their feet and to adapt to the ever changing environment of the physical education gymnasium.

Developmentally Appropriate Modifications

Developmentally appropriate modifications to a lesson can accomplish many objectives such as increasing or decreasing the complexity of the game or activity. Sawicki (2000) showed there are several aspects of activities and games that can be modified to allow for maximum participation and increased success. These include: the rules, the boundaries, the equipment, movement patterns, and special modifications.

One rule change might be to require all players on the same team to touch the ball before someone can score. Or that everyone on the team has to score for the team to win which decreases the chances of better players dominating. Boundaries can be modified by making the activity space larger or smaller or using more goals. One of the most exciting games I have played with students is to have four teams, four soccer nets, and four color jerseys with two soccer balls. Any team can score in any of the other three goals.

Equipment can be modified to meet the developmental level of the students. Using t-ball stands, tennis racquets instead of baseball bats, larger or lighter balls, etc., all can be used to make activities easier and more exciting for the students. Movement patterns can be modified by asking students to skip instead of run, run backwards instead of forward, or use their non-dominant hand. These modifications give the students a different movement and therefore new experiences for controlling their bodies while in activities or games. Special modifications such as setting a time limit or having scoring changes can also be implemented. For example, a badminton game can be played to seven points instead of 15 or extra points can be awarded for a smash (award more points if the skill focus is used). These changes challenge the students to practice under time constraints (as in a traditional sport) or create a situation of excitement by providing new rules for scoring in the game.

There are many reasons to modify activities or games (see Sawicki, 2000). A more comprehensive list and several reasons gleaned from this book to modify activities would be: to increase or decrease complexity of the task being done, decrease boredom, increase or decrease competition level, decrease negative behaviors, promote success, promote social behavior, promote creativity, increase student interest, increase fun and enjoyment for students, increase participation, increase practice time, increase variation in learning a skill, increase teamwork, to meet various physical needs, to meet the developmental level of the students, to meet students cognitive abilities, to adapt to the class size, to adapt to the equipment available, to create a safe environment, to develop specific skills, and to change activities if the class is not going as planned. All or any of these reasons to modify activities or games should be kept in mind by physical education teachers. Using these reasons to modify acitivities or games will undoubtedly lead to excellence in teaching.

Local Public school students join in at the Canisius College Gymnasium

Modifying Equipment

Many physical education equipment rooms do not have the necessary equipment to play the traditional or even a modified version of a game. Teachers can still plan activities and use available equipment or make their own equipment. Teachers have to be creative and not always rely on traditional equipment to plan lessons and activities in the gymnasium. The following is a variety of home built equipment that can service the needs of teachers where equipment is lacking. Chairs or plastic soda bottles can be used as pylons or goals. PVC piping (black plastic piping that is used in plumbing which is often thrown away at construction sites and is very inexpensive) can be used as relay batons or as pylons or goals used to place balls on top. PVC piping can also be used to make traditional goals.

Computer mouse pads and plastic coasters can be used as poly spots. Old t-shirts can be used as pinnies or markers to designate teams. Placing rice, popcorn or beans inside a sock can create a bean bag or hackey sack. Old fabric sewed together and stuffed with beans makes for a great bean bag. Garbage cans, buckets or milk cartons can be used as goals for throwing. Balloons and beach balls are excellent striking objects for elementary students. Soda bottles, especially the larger ones make wonderful goals, pylons and bowling pins. If the soda containers are filled with sand, they stand up more easily and can be used for a variety of needs. To make racquets, a teacher can pull a panty hose around a coat hanger and duct tape the end to ensure no sharp edges are left around the hanger. Small or larger beanie babies and stuffed animals make excellent bean bags for throwing games or as objects to retrieve. Jumping ropes can be made into circles on the floor as designated safety areas as a hula hoop would have done. Jump ropes can create boundary areas that are safe to use, unlike hula hoops which can be dangerous on the gymnasium floor. If the ropes on the floor are stepped on they will not tend to slide. Scoops can be created out of bleach/milk bottles where the top belly is cut out. The handle of the bottle makes a sturdy holder for the scoop. Netting can be made from plastic six pack soda holders tied together with string. Teachers can make yarn balls for throwing made from yarn scraps from around the home. Athletic non-stick tape can make targets on the wall or boundaries on the gymnasium floor. I always tell my students there is virtually no tape that will hold a target on a gymnasium wall (i.e., hula hoop), so using tape directly on the wall to make a target is recommended. Old bed sheets sew together can make a parachute. Golf tubes placed inside a cone can make a t-ball batting stand. Coffee lids can be numbered and used as poly spots or Frisbees.

Whatever equipment the teacher creates and modifies to use in his/her lessons the students will appreciate the extra time and effort. Having students help make the equipment is a great idea and decorating the equipment to suit the students taste is a wonderful way of having the students feel they contributed to your physical education class.

Classroom Management

Establishing rules of behavior for students in the physical education gymnasium is important for good physical education teaching. Physical education teachers should think that their gymnasium is no different a teaching environment then the science, English or math classroom. Posting signs that no food or drink is allowed in the gymnasium and taking pride in the gymnasium as a classroom is one suggested way to let everyone in the school know that the gymnasium is an academic classroom.

At the beginning of each semester students can create a list of rules (behaviors) they would like to follow when taking physical education. Having the students help create the list and using a large poster board displayed in the gymnasium will help with the students commit to the rules more.

An example poster board may be: *PHYSICAL EDUCATION WORKS BEST WHEN:* 1. Students do not talk when the teacher is talking, 2. No jewelry is worn, 3. Students keep hands to ourselves, 4. Students are dressed appropriately, 5. Students do their best in all activities, 6. Students help other students with their skills, 7. We take care of the equipment, 8. We help the teacher with the equipment and set up of equipment, 9. We put away all equipment neatly when class is over, 10. We help other classmates learn the skills.

Gymnasium rules are best created with both the students and the teacher. Having the students help create the list leads to more accountability. In fact, students will monitor each other and make reference to the list to other students if he/she is breaking a rule. When creating the list the teacher has the option to write the students suggestion verbatim or modify it slightly to suit the logistics of the gymnasium.

For example, a student may say to the teacher as a desired rule, 'do not push and shove in the gymnasium,' the teacher may reply 'an excellent suggestion' how about we write it 'keep your hands to yourself.' As a teacher you will quickly see there are common rules that students tend to create and the suggestions they give will undoubtedly fall into common rules.

For good classroom management the teacher should plan how students will move from one place to another to get equipment, move to the next activity station or come into and leave the gymnasium. There are numerous ways to line up students so they can move when the teacher needs them to. Lining up students is an effective way to move students from the gymnasium to the next teacher picking the students up from class.

Some of the more frequently used ways teachers line up students is to say, "Would everyone who …" 1) is wearing a striped shirt line up, then yellow shirt, green shirt, etc., until all students are selected, 2) has a birthday in January, February, March etc., until all months are done, 3) is an odd number age, then even number age, 4) plays a musical instrument, plays a sport, has a pet dog or cat, etc., and 5) can divide 100 by 4, multiply 3 x 3, add 4 +1, etc. Teachers should use a different way to line up their classes each day. This is a fun way to move the students from one area to the next and creates an excellent way to behaviorally manage the class.

Other ways to have students line up are: left side to right side, by age, hair length, birthday (day of the month), foot size, and height. Ways to group students are by shirt color, ability to play musical instruments, first name with two vowels, and put shoes in middle and toss different directions. A teacher needs to be creative and have fun with this and it is all part of good physical education teaching.

Physical Education Standards and Professionalism

Physical education teachers have a unique challenge to present physical education as a physical, social, mental and emotional discipline. National and State Standards can be selected in each lesson plan to allow teachers to teach all domains to the students (called outcomes or goals). Physical education standards have aspects of all domains and it is the job of the teacher to ensure the students develop wholly in all of them.

Standard II

Aside from physical education standards teachers should strive for professionalism in themselves and respect from students taking physical education. One of the recommendations for teachers in physical education is to institute a dress code for students. There are an abundance of reasons why students should change clothes for physical education. By having a dress code the students can experience physical education as a special and unique discipline. Verbal accounts of physical education being a 'glorified recesses' have in some ways been justified because of what we do and how the students mentally view physical education. Having students change for classes may not completely eliminate the perception physical education is similar to recess but it will help downplay that image. I have seen students in physical education wearing jeans, hats and long sleeve shirts and wondered how those students feel about physical education as an academic discipline. Further, having students meet a certain dress code shows that physical education has rules to follow and sets it apart from recess and free play.

When I teach physical education, I have all students dress in shorts and t-shirt (no hats) and there are no allowances for any other uniform. By having a dress code in physical education classes, the students learn to be responsible and prepared when coming to class. If the student shows up unprepared (likened to not having their homework done), I nicely but clearly state, "I am sorry but you have to watch and take notes today and forego the participation grade for today". In all my years of teaching, I have never had a problem with students forgetting their uniform more than once or twice in a semester. Requiring a uniform develops self-discipline, self-respect, and pride in physical education which far outweighs any minor inconvenience it causes.

When instituting a dress code the teacher cannot bend that rule regardless of the circumstance. I say to the students clearly and emphatically, "please do not take it personally but a rule is only a rule if you institute it consistently. If I bend the rule for you then I have to bend the rule for everyone from now on or your fellow students would view me as playing favorites." I may also add that anyone who forgets their uniform, "even though you are a wonderful person and I know you did not forget your uniform on purpose you will have to sit and watch today". It is hard to impose penalties when a student is willing and keen to participate but keeping rules fair and consistent for all students is a must for physical education teachers to maintain respect. Teachers may also take this rule further to add a no hat rule in the classroom to further promote professionalism. I have seen dress codes as extreme as having uniforms in the gymnasium a certain color, design or school logo. A dress code for many reasons is a positive part of any physical education program.

Teacher professionalism is an important aspect of being a good physical education teacher. Physical education teachers have to teach skills but must remember not to engage in activities with students other than for teaching purposes. It is tempting for a teacher to join in activities but this can create many problems. The first and foremost problem is that playing with the students decreases the supervisory abilities of the teacher and therefore creates a libelous legal situation for the teacher. I viewed a soccer class once in which the teacher was dribbling the ball down the field while a large group of students gave chase. Other students decided not to give chase and were doing cartwheels on the sidelines, others were sitting on sidelines watching and yet other students were swinging on the goal posts. The teacher had a total inability to supervise the class while dribbling the soccer ball himself and therefore created a dangerous legal situation which the teacher was responsible for. If a student who is not participating had been hurt (for example there was a case where a student swung on a soccer goal post and it came down and killed the student), the teacher, by law, has no defense as to why he/she was playing and not supervising. At best, in court, there would be high contributory negligence on the part of the teacher towards a student getting hurt where supervision was lacking. Stay Professional, Stay Alert to Safety.

Portfolio Development

Every student in any physical education teacher education program should develop a personal portfolio of academic accomplishments which include: a teaching philosophy, resume and samples of academic work. The personal portfolio can be electronic by downloading it to a website (a student can use one of the many free websites available online like Tasktream.com or Weebly.com) or a hard copy portfolio professionally displayed in a binder using such programs as PowerPoint.

Students can also develop an electronic portfolio which includes: a philosophy statement on teaching, resume, certifications and volunteer work and course assignments to show their content knowledge (National Physical Education Standard) in physical education. Websites such as Taskstream.com or Weebly.com can help facilitate an electronic portfolio development.

Chapter Two

Physical Education Lessons Plans

Included in this book are 20 exciting movement education lesson plans in abbreviated form. The lesson plans are primarily geared towards the Gr.4 to Middle School age group but can be scaled up to teach Middle or High School or down to reach Gr.K-3 ages. Teachers should take principles they have learned from this book and apply them, making detailed verbal commands while using these lessons plans. One book principle that should be applied to these lessons is Think on your Feet, which means adapting and changing these lessons as the situation in the gymnasium warrants.

The 20 lessons of this book are a great starting point to create new and exciting physical education lessons. The lessons provided are loosely geared to a 50-60-minute physical education period but I have used one lesson across many days of physical education. Expanding on what is already included in these 'fail safe' lesson plans will undoubtedly provide many lessons of physical education which can extend to half an academic school year or more. By using the modification principles shown in this book, the teacher will help the lessons suit the developmental level of the students undertaking them.

Lesson #1- First Week Activities

Skill: Loco-motor - Walk, Run, Skip, Gallop

Theme: Space Awareness

Sub-Theme: Pathways (curved, zig zag, straight)

Read: Sawicki, T. M. (2005) or www.humankinetics.com/acucustom/sitename/Documents/D ocumentItem/4894.pdf

Equipment: Yarn balls, colored magic markers, 14" Bristol board strips (1 per student), stop watch, music player and music CD, 10 Frisbees, 10 hoops, 10 wooden pins, 2 red poly spots, and about 20 other colored poly spots and masking tape.

Physical Outcome: Running and various other ways to loco-mote

Social: Teamwork

Emotional/Affective: Communicate and help other students during the activity.

The following activities can be completed in about 50 min.

1. Communication Bingo

Students compete to fill in all the spaces on a previously created 25-square Bingo Communication card. Squares are filled in by finding someone in the class who can answer a square's question and writing that student's name in the square. (See suggested questions for the card below.) Each square on the card must be filled in with a different classmate's name. A fully completed Bingo card wins the game. The teacher can give the Communication Bingo winner an award for his/her excellent communication skills after checking and reading the answers out loud to check for accuracy. If there is no one in the class who can answer one of the questions in a square, students can write "Free" in that space.

		Free		

Communication Bingo Blank Card

Some of the squares might include:

1. Find someone who knows twins

2. Find someone who can make a word with their first name

3. Find someone who has the same birthday month as you

4. Find the youngest person in the class

5. Find the person who lives closest to school

6. Find someone who can name three NFL quarterbacks

7. Find someone who speaks three languages

8. Find someone who has met a movie star

9. Find someone who can name the cast of Gilligan's Island

10. Find someone who knows when the Titanic sank

Bingo cards have 24 squares: five across, five down, with the middle square designated as Free.

Warm Up

2. Jog around the gymnasium to music using different pathways (straight, curved, and zigzag) and locomotion type (i.e., hop, skip, jump, gallop, and slide).

3. Find a starting spot. Stand tall and print your first name on the gym floor using different ways to loco-mote on the gymnasium floor. (Walk in a circle to create an "O", hop in a straight line and then slide side-to-side to create a "T")

4. Everyone used such a small area of the gymnasium! I'd like you to print your name again but do it as large as you can this time. Use the whole gymnasium if you like.

5. Find a partner whose first name you do not know. Play follow-the-leader on the gymnasium floor. Print your first

name again and have your partner attempt to figure it out as you go. Afterward, switch it up and have your partner do the same for you.

6. Once you have figured out each other's names, find new partners and do it all again.

7. Everyone line up in alphabetical order by first name. (Use a line on the gymnasium floor.) First names from A on my left to Z on my right. Time the line-up with a Stopwatch. Call out a "world record" time to beat (i.e., 20 seconds) so students line up as quickly as possible. You can now use this time to have students line up quickly the entire year.

8. Students step forward, turn to your classmates (step out and turn 180 degree), and call out your first name. (Begin with first names, A. This makes sure they are in the right order. It also reinforces classmate names to all students in the class).

9. Next, form a circle of five to six people. Give one yarn ball to each group. The person with the yarn ball will show a stretch. Everyone in the group hold that stretch for ten seconds. Toss the yarn ball to a groupmate while calling out that person's name. That person becomes the next stretch leader.

Skill Development

10. Distribute Bristol board strips (one-inch-wide and 14 inches long) and colored magic markers and masking tape to students. Instruct the students to make a headband with their name on it. Really jazz it up!

11. With your headband on your head, jog in different pathways around the area. (Play music.)

As you jog, say "Hi" to your classmates, give them a high five, and call them by name. If you don't know someone's name, read their headband as you pass by.

12. Now, place all the headbands on the floor. Use different pathways to jog in and out among the headbands. Be careful not to step on one. When the music stops, pick up the headband closest to you and find its owner (Repeat this a several times.).

13. Line up in alphabetical order again (Time it to see if they get faster.).

14. Next, form a circle of five to six people. One person stand in the middle of the circle with a Frisbee. Spin the Frisbee on its edge (like spinning a coin on a table) in the middle of the circle and call the name of someone else in the circle. That person must run around the outside of the circle and enter the circle when they reach the spot they started from. Try to run fast enough to pick up the Frisbee before it stops spinning. This activity can also be tried using hula hoops or wooden pins. **NOTE:** Hula Hoops will stop spinning quickly and can be used with highly-skilled students. Wooden pins spin for a very long time and can be used for students who are at a lower skill level.

Culminating Activity/Game

15. Name Roulette: Form two large circles that almost touch each other (see diagram below). At the point where the circles almost touch, two students will be standing back to back, each facing inside their circle. Use a poly spot to

44

identify where the two circles touch. As music plays, the two circles jog clockwise. Two students continuously pass each other at the poly spot. When the music stops, the two students nearest to the poly spot turn to each other and call out the other's name. Anyone calling out a correct name switches to the other circle. The largest circle (whichever group knew more names) at the end of the game wins.

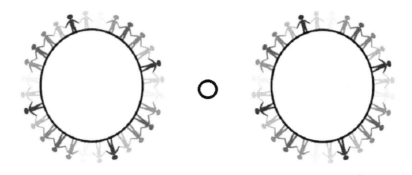

Poly spot

Fun Cognitive Cool Down

16. Come to Lunch with Me: The whole class sits shoulder to shoulder in a circle. Teacher says: "Hi! My name is _____ and I would like all of you to come to lunch with me. I am going to bring _____ (name two items someone might bring to lunch). To come to lunch, you must figure out what you need to bring to join me." This is a problem-solving game. The game requires each student to select two food or drink items that start with the initials of their first and last names. For example, a teacher with the initials T.S. might say, "Hi! My name is Tim Sawicki and I am going to bring Tea and Sandwiches for lunch today." The students do not know the

way to solve the task at the beginning of the game. To begin, the teacher points to a student in the circle and asks if he or she would like to come to lunch. The student replies, "Hi! My name is ____ and I would like to come to lunch with you. I would like to bring _____ (name two items)." If the student names two items that begin with the same letters as their initials, the teacher responds, "Yes, you can come to lunch with me." If the items do not begin with the student's initials, the teacher responds, "Sorry, no, you cannot come to lunch with me." The activity proceeds around the circle clockwise. The teacher should preface the game by informing students that there is a trick to getting the right answer and that they should not take it personally if they are denied coming to lunch. It may also be necessary to include some clues to help students figure out the trick. A nice benefit for the students as the game is played is that they are repeatedly reminded of each other's names.

These first week activities described above are geared to help the teacher get to know the students and the students get to know each other. This breaks down barriers students may have with each other, and knowing one another creates a great atmosphere that is conducive to learning and sharing for the rest of the school year.

So nice to meet you

Lesson #2

Skill: Loco-motor - Run, Skip, Gallop

Theme: Space Awareness

Sub-Theme: Pathways (curved, zig-zag, straight)

Equipment: Music CD, pylons,

Teaching Tips: Safety discussion about tagging classmates (do not tag hard), running technique cues (head up, body erect, eyes looking ahead)

Warm Up

1. Jog through open spaces to the music anywhere in the gymnasium

2. Use all space in the gymnasium, going into the middle and out again

3. Change pathways (curved, zig zag, straight) as you move

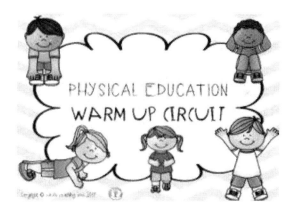

Skill Development

1. Write your first name on the gymnasium floor while moving, have a start and end position

2. Write it as large as you can while moving using all the space

3. Choose a partner but do not introduce yourself. Using all the space follow the leader of one partner, after one partner spells name, guess their name. Now, have the other person lead and then guess their name (Teachers ask: how many pairs guessed both partners' name correctly?)

Game/Culminating Activity

7. Crows and Cranes: Choose a partner and meet at the center of the gymnasium. This forms the two teams. (Partners going to opposite teams is a great way to make two teams). One team is called the Crows and faces the other team that is called Cranes who are on the center line. When the Crows are called, they chase the Cranes toward the pre-designated safety line at one end of the gymnasium while attempting to tag them. When the Cranes are called, they chase the Crows to the safety line while attempting to tag them. When someone is tagged he/she must go to the other team. Students should be reminded to remember which team they are on.

Rule: You can tag anyone on the other team, not just your partner. The team with the most members on their side wins. Implement a time limit or number of turns.

Modifications: Change movement pattern (skip, slide, hop), make up new names for the Crows and the Cranes.

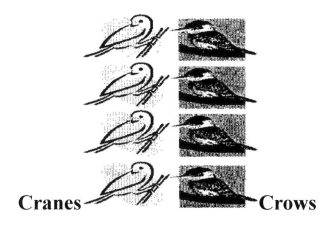

Cranes **Crows**

8. Sharks and Minnows: Two volunteers are chosen to be the catchers (Sharks). The Sharks stand at the center line of half court and wait for the Minnows to swim (run) by. The Sharks catch the Minnows by tagging them. If caught, the Minnow turns to Seaweed at the spot he/she was tagged. Seaweed can help the Sharks by swaying their arms to the left and right as uncaught Minnows swim by. The Minnows' goal is to make it untagged to the pre-designated safety area.

Rule: Once you are caught and become Seaweed, you must stay in place and only move your arms.

Modifications: Change the loco-motor movements of the Sharks or Minnows. Create new names for the Sharks and Minnows. Add a one-step limit for the Seaweed.

Lesson #3

Skill: Loco-motor - Run, Skip, Hop

Theme: Space Awareness

Sub-Theme: Directions (Forward, Backwards, Sideways)

Equipment: Pylons, skipping ropes, beanbags, socks, Velcro straps or any straps

Teaching Tips: Safety discussion

Warm Up

1. Snake Alive: The whole class stands beside one student who is chosen by the teacher to be the main Snake. That student lies face down on the gymnasium floor. When the teacher calls "Snake alive!" the Snake attempts to tag as many students as possible by twirling on the ground. Once a student is tagged, he/her becomes a Snake too. The next round starts by everyone once again standing beside the main Snake. When "Snake alive!" is called again, the uncaught students must weave in and out of all the Snakes to get to safety. Play continues until all students are caught.

2. Loco-mote with a skipping rope around the gymnasium.

50

Skill Development

3. Loco-mote with a skipping rope around the gymnasium, moving forward, backward, sideways.

4. Two people travel with one rope changing directions.

5. Groups of four. Tie two ropes together, practice skipping. Work on ways to enter the rope with two classmates twirling the rope.

6. Jake the Snake: Tie a bean bag to the end of the rope. Using the same group of four as previous activity, gather around the person holding the snake. That person swings the rope around themselves while the rest of the group members hop over it as it goes under them. If those students hop too late and the snake wraps around him/her, that person takes over the snake in the center.

Hint: The person in the middle should not just spin 360 degrees or he/she will get dizzy. Instead, pass the snake from one hand to another around the body.

Culminating Activity/Game

7. Tail Tag 2: Each student gets a rope and tucks it into the back of his/her shorts so it hangs down like a tail. The tail must be dragging along the floor. The students run around the gymnasium with tails dragging behind. When the teacher calls "Go!" the students try to step on each other's tails.

Rule: You have to keep jogging at all times even if another student steps on your tail. Once your tail has been stepped on, and it comes out of your shorts, you pick up the rope and skip with it until all players are done. A winner is declared when there is only one player left with the tail in his/her shorts.

Lesson #4

Skill: Loco-motor - Run, Skip, Hop

Theme: Space Awareness

Sub-Theme: Directions (Forward, Backwards, Sideways)

Equipment: Pylons, short skipping ropes, or Velcro straps

Teaching Tips: Safety discussion

Warm Up

1. Students are asked to touch all four walls of the gymnasium traveling forward, backward, and sideways. The teacher will explain there is an easy way to accomplish the task.

Hint: Running to one corner of the gymnasium and placing both hands, one on each corner, and then running to the other diagonal corner of the gymnasium and placing both hands, one on each corner, is the fastest and easiest way complete this task. You might present a "MENSA" award if a student does this on the first try.

2. Pylons are placed in a square around the gymnasium. Students are divided into four groups and one group is lined up at each pylon. The teacher calls "Go!" and the first student in each line runs to the next group in a forward run. Once there, the next student in line runs. Students are asked to run first forward, then backward, then sideways no matter which pylon he/she is at. Five minutes of time is counted by the teacher as warm up time and all students run clockwise.

3. Stretch: Students form a circle in which to stretch, i.e., the tallest student holds the first stretch for 10 seconds, and then the next person in the circle (going clockwise) creates the next stretch. Stretching continues for two trips around the circle.

Skill Development

3. Catch a Fish: Two students are designated as the Catchers. The Catchers hold hands (or wrists, or two Velcro straps connected between them) to create their net and run around

the gymnasium and try to catch (tag and ensnare) as many Fish as possible.

Rule: Caught Fish become part of the net. Fish cannot break through the net as they're being caught, but if the net stretches and breaks, those Fish are freed. The net keeps growing bigger and bigger by tagging new Fish and adding them on to the net ends.

Hint: The strategy of the net should be to huddle and decide on one Fish for everyone to catch. This should help avoid the net breaking.

The game ends when everyone in the class becomes part of the net and is holding hands. At that point, the teacher can state, "Now that is what I call class Togetherness!"

4. Sharks and Barracudas: Half the class is designated as the Barracudas and the other half are designated as Sharks. The Sharks face the wall. The Barracudas sneak up on the Sharks and attempt to tag them. The teacher calls, "Sharks are coming!" and the Sharks turn from the wall and chase the Barracudas to a safety line. If caught, the student goes to the opposite team.

Hint: Students should be reminded to remember which team (Sharks or Barracudas) they are on.

Lesson #5

Skill: Loco-motor - Running

Theme: Body Awareness

Sub-Theme: Body Parts (identifying Body Parts)

Equipment: Pylons, beanbags

Teaching Tips: Safety discussion, music CD

Warm Up

1. Simon Sez: Works on recognition of body parts. My Simon Sez expert approach - The teacher says "Is everyone ready to go?" Anyone who responds is out. Teachers says, "Everyone spread out, take a step away from others." Anyone who moves is out. Now the game can begin.

2. Jog around the gymnasium to the music using all the space.

3. Travel using different ways and different body parts, i.e., hop, cartwheel.

4. When the teacher calls out a body part, the student touches that part to the floor and then continues on jogging. Include the back which requires the students to perform a roll. Teacher will demonstrate a safe roll.

5. Stretch with a partner connecting different body parts.

Skill Development

6. People to People: Students move around the gymnasium to the music. The teacher calls out a body part ("People to People, i.e., left foot!").

Students must find a partner quickly and connect those two parts. The last two students to connect or a student who does not find a partner (odd number left) calls out the next part. After a few rounds with partners, move on to groups of three, then groups of four, etc., all connecting the same way as they did with partners. Culminate with the whole class in the center of the gymnasium connecting one chosen body part.

Hint: The student calling out "People to People!" must remember to connect with someone or as a consequence he/she will remain caller.

7. All students get a bean bag. Throw the bean bag and catch on the body part the teacher calls out. Throw bean bag in the air, turn 180 degrees, and then catch it. Throw bean bag in the air and clap before catching it, etc.

8. Students walk around the designated area with the bean bags on their heads. If the bean bag falls off, you are frozen. To unfreeze, a classmate has to pick the bean bag up for you and put it back on your head. The teacher asks the students to increase the speed of walking up to a jog, change direction, etc. The classmate who helps unfreeze the most students wins the Friendship award.

Culminating Activity/Game

9. Body Part Relay: Divide the class into five lines of six people. Each group lines up at a pylon and then three members of each group goes to a pylon at the other end of the gymnasium.

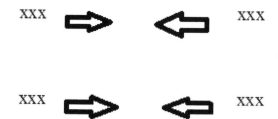

Starting with the left sideline, each player is given a number and body part. For example, player #1 (first in the left line) is given the body part shoulder. Player #2 in the same line is given a different body part (i.e., right arm). Follow that process until all six students in the two lines have a number and a body part. The line across also are given the same numbers (#1- first person in line, shoulder, etc.). You can use poster board if you'd like so students can see the order of body parts carrying the bean bag.

One line's body part order: (#1) shoulder, (#2) right arm, (#3) back, (#4) left leg, (#5) head, (#6) right foot.

Each team gets one bean bag. Player #1 places the bean bag on their shoulder and when the teacher says "Go!" Player #1 races across the gymnasium to the other group members and gives the bean bag to player #1 in the line across the gymnasium. That player #1 takes the bean bag and places it on his/her shoulder and heads back to the other line and hands it off to player #2. Player #2 puts the bean bag on their designated body part and crosses to the other line. The relay continues until all teams are finished. 12 players in total.

Rule: If the bean bag falls off the body part, the player stops and puts it back and continues on. Players must sit down when they complete their leg of the relay.

10. Frozen Body Part Tag: Taggers wear pinnies. When a player is tagged the first time, the player holds the body part that was tagged and keeps running. If tagged a second time, the player is frozen and assumes a frog position. Players that are not caught can unfreeze players by doing a leap frog over them. This is a never ending game. Switch taggers wearing the pinnies every few minutes.

Pinnies used to designate taggers
Unfreeze a Caught Classmate

Lesson #6

Skill: Running and Jumping

Theme: Space Awareness

Sub-Theme: Pathways (Curved, Straight, Zig-zag)

Equipment: Pylons, pinnies (shirt markers), beanbags, poly spots, footballs, Velcro straps

Teaching Tips: Safety discussion

Warm Up

1. Teach and practice ways of jumping - one foot to one foot, a leap which is one foot to opposite foot, two feet to two feet, two feet to one foot.

2. Whole class stretch. Ask for a student volunteer. (i.e., an athlete.) Use music.

Skill Development

3. Jack Frost/Jane Thaw: Two students are designated as Jack Frost (taggers) and two or three students are designated as Jane Thaw (thawers). When a student is tagged, they freeze in a frog shape. Jane Thaw unfreeze by leaping over the frozen player.

Culminating Activity/Game

4. Capture the Bean Bag: Divide the class into two teams by numbering one, two, one, two. Which team wears the pinnies is decided by one player on each teach playing Paper, Rocks, and Scissors. A center line is marked with two pylons. There is a Holding Pen area and a beanbag area at one end of the gymnasium/field (see diagram below). Teams attempt to capture the five bean bags from the other team and bring them back to their side without getting tagged. There is a safety area (crease/dead zone) around the holding pen area and a safety area (crease/dead zone) around the bean bag area which no one can go in unless capturing a bean bag or freeing tagged players.

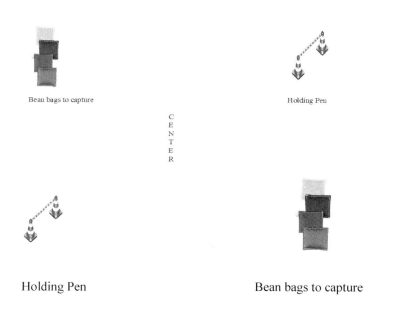

Bean bags to capture   Holding Pen

C
E
N
T
E
R

Holding Pen   Bean bags to capture

Play continues until one team has captured all five bean bags and brought them back to their side of the gymnasium. This is an excellent game to be played outdoors.

Culminating Activity/Game

Capture the Football: Instead of bean bags like the previous game, use footballs in a hoop at each end where the bean bags would have been. Teams have flags hanging from their sides (like in flag football). Instead of being tagged, a flag is pulled from the player's side. A team must make three passes to get the football to their side of center to score a point. Play a game to ten points. The safety area (dead zone/crease) as in Capture the Beanbag circle area around the footballs (see below).

Lesson #7

Skill: Throwing, Running

Theme: Space Awareness

Sub-Theme: Levels (High, Medium, Low)

Equipment: Pylons, variety of 100 objects (small balls, beanie babies, bean bags)

Teaching Tips: Safety discussion, teach throwing technique (show five points on Bristol board that teaches throwing, i.e., stance, transfer of weight, follow-through, etc.)

Warm Up

1. Take It Back: Divide the class into four teams. Place four pylons in a square around the gymnasium. Each team goes to one of four pylons. A group of objects (bean bags, small balls, beanie babies) are placed in a hoop in the middle of the square. One player from a team runs up and takes an object and brings it back to their next teammate in line, throwing it to him/her. Once the object is caught and placed on the ground, the next person in line takes his/her turn. When all objects have been picked up, each team counts how many objects have been retrieved. The team with the most objects is the winner. An award is given for Take It Back Champions.

2. Stretch using one ball between two people, stretch with the ball.

Skill Development

3. Work on the technique of throwing in partners with a single line across the gymnasium (use any type of ball).

4. Change the ways partners throw, i.e., throw up to the ceiling (works on accuracy).

5. Throw low. This gets the student into a baseball pitcher stance. Throw five times each.

6. Throw a bounce pass and have it land in the partner's chest (numbers).

7. Throw to the partner so he/she has to make an over-the-head catch.

8. Groups of two with one quarterback and one receiver. The receiver runs out, does a pattern, and then catches the ball thrown by the quarterback.

9. Groups of four. Cover the quarterback and receiver. Switch after a count of five Mississippi.

Culminating Activity/Game

10. Relay Over and Under: Divide the class into five groups. Each group stands in a line at the end of the gymnasium. The first person in each line gets a playground ball and all other players behind the first player opens their legs to form a tunnel (see diagram below). The last player in line bends over and looks through the tunnel of legs. When the teacher says "Go!" the first player throws/rolls the ball between all the legs to the last player in line.

Rule: The ball must go through all the players' legs or your team is disqualified. The last player in the line receives the ball and runs to a spot about three steps ahead of the front of the line. The teams continue to move down the gymnasium to a designated spot finish line. The first team to have all members cross the finish line and sitting wins the race.

Relay #2: Toss the ball over the head backwards to next player in line. Same set up as above.

Relay #3: Toss the ball under then over to the next player in line. Same set up as above. Have a Cooperation award for the winning team.

Lesson #8

Skill: Throwing, Running

Theme: Space Awareness

Sub-Theme: Levels (High, Medium, Low)

Equipment: Pylons, variety of objects (small balls, beanie babies, bean bags)

Teaching Tips: Safety discussion, teach throwing technique (show 5 points on bristol board. stance, transfer of weight, follow-through, etc.)

Read: Sawicki, T. M. (2002)

While teaching in college, my students and I developed an active, high-spirited game that my classes have enjoyed for many years. I have used this game while teaching K-12 students right through to college level. The games allows for developmentally appropriate competition for any age group. The game is called Feed the Penguin and has stood the test of time.

The game uses the word "penguin" as a representation of a ball resting on top of a pylon.

A Penguin

We play several games with the word "penguin" in the title, such as Protect the Penguin and Capture the Penguin. All the games with "penguin" in the title refer to a ball on top of a pylon.

Feed the Penguin is a combination of popular team games like basketball, handball and hockey. Feed the Penguin and the preliminary lead up activities are excellent for practicing the fundamental skills of throwing, catching, and running. Developmentally appropriate modifications (Sawicki, 2000) are used to change the level of difficulty of the game to suit the abilities of students, i.e., changing the boundary size, balls, rules and height of the penguin.

Warm Up

Catching and throwing activities can be developed in each lead up activity and by extending the catching and throwing elements from stationary to moving, i.e., throw while running as opposed to throwing while stationary.

1. Set up three penguins and have the participants throw from designated distances (three feet, six feet, nine feet, etc.) to knock over the first one, then a second, and then the third penguin which is farthest away. Teams of small groups are formed and score is kept using the highest total of balls knocked off the penguin. The closest penguin is one point, the second farthest is two points, and knocking the ball off the third and farthest penguin is three points. A group of three players might score as high as 18 points if all three players hit the ball off each of the three penguins. A time limit can he introduced to encourage running while throwing. Objects on top of the penguin can be modified to engage players at varied developmental levels, i.e., larger sponge balls for younger groups or smaller tennis or ping pong balls for older groups. The object thrown can he modified to increase complexity too, such as throwing a Frisbee rather than a ball. Finally, the distance of the line of penguins can be modified to change levels of difficulty. Lead up activities

that provide practice in the fundamental skills of running, throwing and catching in a variety of situations prepare the participants for the more complex activities of Protect the Penguin and Feed the Penguin. With the modifications listed in this book, teachers can easily create many different skill development activities in this lesson.

Culminating Activity/Games – Protect the Penguin and Feed the Penguin

2. A lead up game called Protect the Penguin is one that can be used for children of all ages. A group of children circle around a penguin being guarded by another player. A ball (a playground or softer ball) is passed around a circle and when open, a player throws the ball at the penguin, attempting to knock it off. One player moves like a hockey goalie to protect the penguin. The student protecting the penguin must take care not to bump it and knock the ball off. Bumping the penguin and having the ball fall off means the protector is out and has to move to a thrower position. The student who threw the ball that knocked the ball off the penguin then becomes goalie. The object of the game is to see how long a player can Protect the Penguin. A built-in safety feature of Protect the Penguin is that the pylon is lower than waist level so the throws are always toward the ground. Players naturally have their hands in from of their bodies also while crouching, and students learn quickly that it is not how hard the ball is thrown but how quickly the player can receive and release the ball towards an open penguin.

3. Feed the Penguin begins by dividing into teams of four to six players on each side. One team plays against another team like in handball, basketball, or hockey. Depending on

class size, the teacher may have several games of Feed the Penguin happening across the gymnasium at one time. I remember teaching high school and we had two games of Feed the Penguin going across the gymnasium and one game being played on the stage above the gymnasium with a smaller group. Needless to say, anyone walking in to the gymnasium would have seen every inch of the space being used with actively moving students. Colored pinnies are used to identify teams and team names may be used for each group of players. Although sitting a team or teams out is not recommended, I have found that the game is so active that having one or two teams rest and watch the action before resuming playing does not detract from the high level activity of an entire class period. A moment of rest is actually appreciated by teams. Rotating teams is fine in this case. Feed the Penguin requires two penguins set up at each end of the gymnasium. Use the basketball free throw circle as a "goalie only" area and place the penguin in the center.

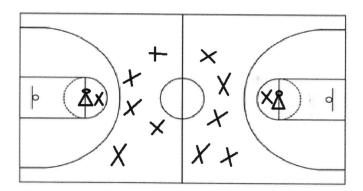

A goalie may be appointed but is not required. Two randomly chosen players on each team jump ball at center as in basketball. Once in possession the team passes a ball

71

down the court or field (if playing outside) and attempts to knock the ball off the penguin.

Rules:

1. The ball does not have to be bounced but players will undoubtedly do this because of their basketball familiarity.

2. There should be no physical contact. Possession is gained by intercepting the ball.

3. An "all touch" rule is in play meaning every player on the team must touch the ball before scoring. You can make this three players, or four players, etc. The team whose four to six players score a certain number of goals wins the game (I have found five goals is a good number).

Feed the Penguin can lead to lots of combinations of teams playing against each other. Awards and certificates can be given to students to signify their participation in Feed the Penguin tournaments. The experiences I have had while supervising Feed the Penguin is that the games propagate a friendly rivalry among the students. As an instructor, the teacher needs to move from one Feed the Penguin game to another to ensure safety. The teacher may even want to call penalties (time-outs) for infractions he/she may see (i.e., light physical contact).

Feed the Penguin is a great outdoor game and allows for many games to be going at once. Outdoors is a prime location for a Feed the Penguin tournament. During my high school teaching, some of the students organized a school-wide Feed the Penguin tournament. Players from different grade levels were placed on different teams to play in the tournament. It was an astounding success and demonstrates the amount of enjoyment students have when playing Feed the Penguin.

I have found while playing Feed the Penguin that students take pride in the team they are on and high-fives are encouraged toward your team and against opponents. In any case, students always have a smile on their face while playing. The smiles are because Feed the Penguin allows for a large range of modifications to suit the age group playing.

Lesson #9 - Special Day Activity - Parachute Activities

Skill: Emotional/Affective Domain: Cooperation, Teamwork, Listening

Equipment: Parachutes, variety of objects (small balls, beanie babies, plastic golf balls), golf tubes, badminton birds, beach balls

Teaching Tips: Safety discussion when using parachute, discipline, teamwork

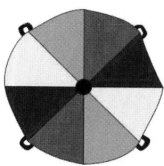

1. Choose a friend and meet at the center of the gymnasium. One partner goes to one side of the gymnasium and the other partner goes to the opposite side. (This allows for friends to be separated and allows for meeting new classmates.) This

process divides the class into two groups, one on each half of the gymnasium. Each group opens up the parachute on their side of the gymnasium (Don't forget to discuss safety, listening, teamwork, etc.).

2. Each group takes the parachute in their right hands and creates small ripples.

3. Switch to left hands and continue to making ripples.

4. Create larger ripples using both hands.

5. Move clockwise raising and lower the parachute using one hand. This is called Merry go Round. Change the movement to hop, skip, gallop, change direction.

6. Next, lift the parachute all together and kneel on it. Punch the parachute in and out with your hands, using it like a punching bag (lots of fun).

7. Lift the parachute all together and everyone release the parachute at the same time. The parachute flies to the ceiling and looks like a mushroom cloud. Watch it float down. Teamwork makes this work. The first few times it will float awkwardly to one side if one side does not release at exact time the others do. It takes some practice all releasing at same time.

8. Next, lift the parachute together and pull down behind your back as you sit inside the parachute. This makes a giant tent and all students sit inside looking at each other.

9. Lift the parachute together and pull down over your neck as you lay down on your stomach. The teacher asks, "Who can make the funniest face?"

10. Mouse Trap: Number everyone in the circle/group around the parachute, i.e., 1-15. Teacher calls the first number randomly as the group raises the parachute. The player with that number runs from one side of the parachute to the other. The group tries to trap the player before he/she gets to the other side. That person gets to call the next number. Teacher must have a safety discussion. Be mindful as you run to the other side because you will be running close to classmates' legs. Avoid running into any classmate legs as you get to the other side of the parachute.

11. Place one ball (beach ball) on the parachute. The class pulls the parachute and watches the ball fly into the air. Add more beach balls. Bounce the balls around. Explain to the students the goal is to keep the ball from rolling off your side of the parachute.

12. Place two balls on the parachute. Keep them from touching. This takes great teamwork.

13. Place a playground ball on the parachute and work to get the ball to lightly touch the ceiling. **Teaching Tip:** Teamwork explanation - take care in how hard the ball hits the ceiling and avoid hitting any lights on the gymnasium ceiling.

14. Popcorn: Bounce a variety of balls on the parachute, i.e., larger soft balls, small plastic golf balls, ping pong balls, etc.

15. Popcorn 2: Place the badminton birds in the parachute and shake them. This looks spectacular.

16. Guard and Protect: Students gather around one parachute. One student lines up behind another student so you have groups of two around the parachute. Bounce plastic golf tubes on the parachute using both hands. The person behind the parachute-holding student keeps the player in front from getting hit with the flying golf tubes. The behind-

student is the protector to the front student. Continue play until all golf tubes are shaken off the parachute.

17. Sharks and Lifeguards: All students go back in their two groups or make two new groups. One group on each side of the gymnasium. Assign one student as a shark and one student as a lifeguard for each group. The students sit with the parachute covering their legs and start by making small ripples with both hands. The Shark goes under the parachute and swims (crawls) around. The Shark grabs the ankles of one student whose legs are under the parachute and attempts to pull him/her into the water (under the parachute). The student calls for help and the Lifeguard runs to his/her aide by grabbing him/her under the armpits pulling them away from the Shark. If a student gets pulled under he/she becomes the new Shark. Switch the Lifeguard every few turns. More than one Shark can be under the parachute but this greatly increases the difficulty of Lifeguards saving the students. Discuss safety related to Sharks pulling the students under (i.e., if the Shark feels the pull-back, he/she must move on to another student).

18. Everyone folds up the parachute(s) together at the end of class. Teamwork discussion.

Lesson #10

Skill: Throwing, Running

Theme: Space Awareness

Sub-Theme: Levels (High, Medium, Low)

Equipment: Pylons, basketballs, nerf balls, yarn balls, foam balls, sponge balls

Teaching Tips: Safety discussion, teach throwing technique (show 5 points on Bristol board- stance, transfer of weight, follow-through, etc.)

Warm Up

1. Divide the class into groups of four to five. Designate one person as the tagger. Three to four players hold wrists, with the tagger on the outside. Appoint one person as tagging target. The tagger attempts to tag the target. The group spins and turns to keep the tagger away from tagging the target. The student to be tagged is at the end of the line. When the Target is tagged, switch places.

Tagger   Group   Target Tagged

Skill Development

2. Globetrotters: In a circle of five throw ball high or bounce it and follow your pass. Pass and run.

3. Three vs. Three Keep Away: Divide up in to equal ability groups of three. All Touch rule may be requested.

Culminating Activity/Game

4. Firing Squad: Discuss the use of players as human targets and the debate that is ongoing. Two players are designated as the throwers. The throwers have all the objects to throw at the players who are running from one end of the gymnasium to the other (see diagram below) All players, except the two throwers are running from one safety line to another across the gymnasium floor. the two players designated are on opposite sidelines with the group running in-between them. The teacher calls "Go!" and the players run from one end of the gymnasium to the other. The two throwers on the sideline throw the balls at the running players attempting to hit them to get them out.

Rule: Once hit the player joins the original throwers on the sidelines and throws at the players who have been not hit yet. Throws must be below the waist. Only Nerf and light balls are used. Play continues until all players are on the sidelines. I have tried yarn balls and bringing the sidelines in closer but the yarn balls do not fly fast enough and the runners do not feel the yarn ball when they get hit. Throwing Nerf balls below the waist can work well.

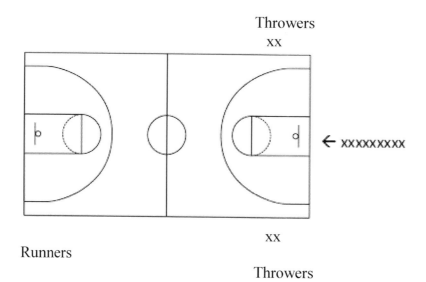

Throwers
xx

← xxxxxxxxx

xx

Runners

Throwers

5. Roll It In: Divide the class into two teams which start on either side of the gymnasium. Players must all stand behind a line (called goal line) at either end of the gymnasium. Each player has a ball. Two basketballs are placed in the center of the gymnasium floor (see diagram below). Players throw their ball at the two basketballs and attempt to have them roll towards the other team's goal which is at the other end. **Rules:** The defending team cannot stop a basketball from rolling into their goal except by throwing one of their balls at it. No one can throw from inside the dead zone/safety area (the area between the goals and in front of each team - similar to the goalie box in a game like soccer). If either basketball rolls outside the play area, it is rolled (straight across) back into play from the sidelines at a slow pace. Players can retrieve balls from the dead zone but must back up behind their goal line to throw.

Safety: Keep heads and eyes up. All throws must be below the waist (30 second penalty for high throws). The game is played until one team scores five goals.

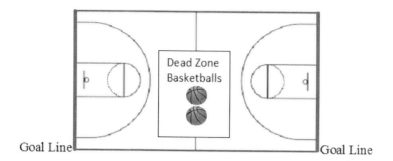

Goal Line ———————————————————— Goal Line

6. Bombardment: The set-up is the same as above but pylons with balls on top are used (Penguins). The penguins are set up across the goal line. The objective is to knock balls off the other team's pylons at the other end of the gymnasium. Same rules apply as Roll It In. Players cannot stop a ball from being knocked off the Penguin. Players must throw the ball below waist level or receive a penalty for high throws. Rolling/bowling is suggested. Once all the balls are off the other team's Penguin a winner is declared. The teacher can also set up wooden pins across the goal line instead of penguins.

Culminating Activity/Game

7. Snowball: Same set up as two above games. All players have a ball. The teacher calls "Go!" and players throw their balls to the other side of the gymnasium. Play continues for three minutes. Same rules as above related to below the waist throws. All throws below waist level. Players may retrieve

balls inside the dead zone and back up to their goal line and throw.

Rule: At the end of the three minutes, no more balls can be thrown. If any are thrown after three minutes, the team is disqualified. The team with the least amount of balls on their side of the gymnasium wins. Frantic but fun game which mimics a snowball fight.

Lesson #11

Skill: Throwing

Theme: Effort Qualities

Sub-Theme: Fine and Firm

Equipment: Variety of playground sized balls (foam, sponge, nerf and playground)

Teaching Tips: Safety discussion, reinforce throwing technique and teach jump shot technique

Warm Up

1. Shuttle Run: Divide the class into groups to five or six. The last person in line sprint's to the head of the line. This continues for 5 minutes. Groups run the perimeter of the

gymnasium/playing field. It is recommended the groups jog very slowly so the last person in line can sprint to the head of the line.

Skill Development

2. Spud/Barney: With the groups of five or six already created previously, number each player, i.e., 1-6. Give one player a ball. The player with the ball stands in the middle of all group members. The middle player throws the ball high in the air and calls a number (other than their own). The player whose number is called runs to the middle catches the ball and calls "Freeze!" When the ball is thrown in the air, all players scatter in every direction away from the middle. Once "Freeze!" is called all players must freeze in their spots. The player whose number is called throws/rolls the ball at the closest player in an attempt to hit them. If he/she misses, a letter of the word "Barney" is verbally given to that player. If the thrower succeeds in hitting the frozen player, the frozen player verbally gets the first letter from the word "Barney". The player who gets a letter calls the next number. Play continues until the word "Barney" is collected by one player. (Feel free to create another word instead of "Barney"). As a teaching tip, it is recommended the game stop before one player gets all the letters.

Rule: The ball must strike a player below the waist.

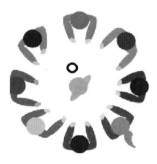

Modification: The player throwing towards another player is allowed to take three steps towards the player they want to hit.

3. Bump/Knockout: Same teams as above. Two playground balls are used and players shoot from the foul line or closer (a new designated line) into the basketball hoop. The player at the start of the line shoots the ball and if he/she misses, shoots again. The second player in line has a chance to bump/knock out the player ahead if he/she makes it before the player directly in front of him/her takes the second shot. If the player in front makes the shot, the ball is passed to the third player in line, who can then bump/knockout the second player. Play continues until all but one player has been knocked out. That player is the winner. Once out, students can move to a consolation game and begin play there.

Culminating Activity/Game

4. Line Basketball (Sawicki, 2006): Pair up students with equal basketball ability. Form two lines across from each other (see diagram below). Number the players on either side, i.e., 1-15. Player's across from each other will have the same number. Every player will have a number forming two teams, i.e., each team has numbers 1-15. Line up on the basketball court sideline across from the player on the other team with the same number. Two balls are placed in the center of the lines.

The teacher calls the first number randomly (#1-15). The two players whose number is called run into the center and each pick up a basketball. The players take the basketball and pass to each team member. One team goes in one direction the other team goes in the other direction toward an open basket. Once the players have passed to all teammates, he/she takes a shot at the basket from outside the key. The first player to make a basket scores a point for his/her team. If the player misses a shot, the ball is re-shot from outside the key and the player keeps shooting until he/she makes the basket. After one basket is made, the point ends and both balls are returned to the center. The player who did not get the point calls the next number (but cannot call their own number). Play continues until one team gets 10 points. That means up to 19 shooting plays (a score of 10-9) so everyone in the class should get a chance = 38 players will have a turn). If there is an odd number, the teacher can compete against the odd numbered student who does not have a partner. This makes a fun class environment where the teacher competes with the class. It is not recommended that the teacher participates in activities with the class often, but in this case the teacher participation allows for good teacher supervision.

Modification: Dribble in and out of each player in line before shooting at the basket.

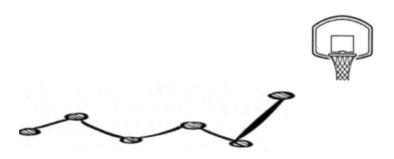

Next bounce pass to each player in the line before shooting at the basket.

5. Culminating Activity/Game

Frog and the Lily Pads (Sawicki, 2005)

Skills: Running, Loco-motor - Hopping and Throwing

Equipment: Numbered poly spots, frog bean bags, basket

Physical outcomes: Loco-motor activities and Throwing

Social outcomes: Teamwork Strategies
Cognitive outcomes: Mathematics/Addition.
Set Up:

Place a basket, i.e., garbage can, or milk crate, or bucket, in the middle of the gymnasium for students to throw the frogs (bean bags) into.

Place numbered poly spots around the basket, with lower numbers closer to the basket and higher numbers further away.

Divide students into teams of five to six. Students line up facing the pond (the basket with the numbered ploy spots scattered around it). The students are the frogs and must hop to a poly spot and throw a frog bean bag into the pond (basket). If the bean bag lands in the basket, the student picks up the poly spot, retrieves the bean bag from the basket, runs back to the team, and passes the bean bag to the next person in line. If the bean bag misses the basket, the student simply retrieves the bean bag and passes it to the next person. Play continues until all the numbered poly spots have been picked up. Typically, the higher number poly spots are remaining as the end of the game approaches. When all numbered poly spots have been picked up, each team sums/counts the poly spots totals they retrieved to determine their total points. This determines a winner for each round. After several rounds, the teams can add those points together for a cumulative total. The teacher can establish a Frog and the Lily Pad World Record for future challenges. Awards or certificates can also be handed out.

Discussion

1. What do you need to think about in order to make very accurate throws? Discuss: Throwing technique cues, force production, direction, etc.

2. What skills did you use to add up the poly spots? (Did they have to use paper and pencil or could they do it in their heads?)

3. What strategy might your team use to try for a new world record? (Lower skilled throwers should make short throws and higher skilled throwers should make longer throws. Or, begin with shorter throws to get many low-value poly spots quickly. Or, make all long throws to get higher-value spots.) Discuss the pros and cons of each strategy.

Lesson #12

Skill: Throwing

Theme: Effort Qualities

Sub-Theme: Fine and Firm

Equipment: Variety of playground sized balls, music CD, pylons, and targets for shooting into (i.e. garbage cans, milk cartons), numbered paper (#1-18 golf holes), masking tape

Teaching Tips: Safety discussion, teach jump shot

Warm Up

1. All students get a ball and stand under a basket outside the key. When the music starts the students takes a shot at one basket from outside the key. If the student misses, he/she retrieves the ball and takes another shot outside key and keeps shooting until it goes in. When a shot goes in from outside the key, the student moves to the next basket. As the music plays, move to each basket around the gymnasium taking shots. Students see how many baskets can be made during the three-minute song. Shooting outside the key is required and no lay-up shots are allowed. Any ball can be used (the better basketball players are asked to use playground or volleyballs to increase difficulty level). A World Record (how many baskets are made) is offered by the teacher to add a challenge to the task.

Note: If the gymnasium has only 2 basketball hoops, add in garbage cans or milk cartons along the sidelines as baskets (see diagram).

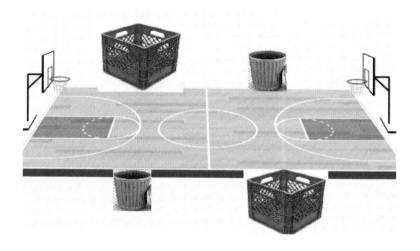

Skill Development

2. Students stretch using one ball.

3. Teacher teaches the technique of the jump shot, i.e., v shape of fingers over forehead, hand in cookie jar to finish, etc.

4. With a partner students go to different baskets practicing jump shots from various distances.

5. Play bump/knockout or line basketball as done on previous lessons but this time use a jump shot instead of a free throw.

Culminating Activity/Game

6. Basketball Golf: Baskets are placed around the gymnasium, i.e., garbage cans, milk cartons or Penguins (ball on a pylon) are place around the gymnasium. The teacher forms partners by pairing the strongest basketball player with the weakest (from the teacher's own observations - does not have to be exact pairings of ability). This continues through all the students in the class. If there is an odd number, the teacher is paired with the last student. Eighteen pylons with a number taped on them are placed at random distances around all the baskets. An equal number of pylons are placed at each basket. The teacher can vary the distance the pylon is placed from the basket depending on the ability of the students.

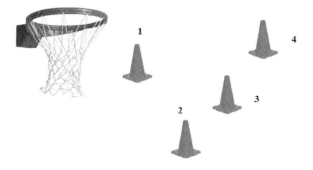

Partners take one scorecard and bring a pencil and one ball to shoot.

		1	2	3	4	5	6	7	8	9	10	11	Total
●	Mall	1	4	2									7
●	Kelly	2	3	2									7
●	Ever	2	3	2									7
●	Ryan	1	3	3									7
●	Molly	4	2	1									7

The pairs of students are asked to go to one basket and start shooting (students can go to any number basket, i.e., a team could start on hole #14). Music is played and students go to any basket and each partner takes a shot at the basket from behind the numbered pylon until the ball goes in.

Rule: Students must shoot from behind the pylon and a limit of five shots on any one hole is the maximum recordable score. On the fifth shot, the score is recorded as five whether making or missing the fifth shot. After all 18 holes are completed by both partners the scorecard is totaled for individual students and as a team. A grand total is recorded on the scorecard and the students hand in their scorecard to the teacher and wait for the announcement of the winning team (low score). A second place and third place team is also announced. A Basketball Golf Award certificate is given to the winning team.

Lesson #13

Skill: Throwing

Theme: Effort Qualities

Sub-Theme: Fine and Firm

Equipment: Frisbees, 21 pylons, whiffle or tennis balls, 30 batons and lummi sticks

Teaching Tips: Safety discussion, teach Frisbee throwing technique (wrist action, transfer of weight, building torque (recoil)

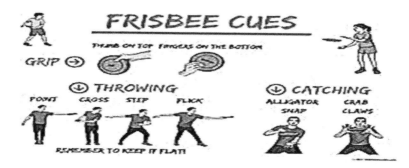

Warm Up

1. Students get a partner and toss the Frisbee across the gymnasium to each other. All students stand side by side who are in the same line.

Skill Development

2. Egg Toss: Students get a partner and toss the Frisbee across the gymnasium to their partner who is 10 feet away. On the teacher's command, one line takes a step back. If the Frisbee is dropped, the players are eliminated and go behind all players to the empty gymnasium space and practice

93

throwing and catching. Play continues until one pair of partners is left and they are declared the class winners of the Egg Toss.

3. Frisbowl: The students are divided into groups of three. Three Penguins (ball on top of pylon) are set up for each group. Each player in the group of three gets a turn at throwing a Frisbee at the three targets. The player can gain three points by hitting all three targets. Each player plays three rounds and tries for a total score out of nine possible points. Since each player can score nine points, and there are three players in a group, a team possible total is out of 27 points. Pylons should be set up at different distances therefore requiring different effort qualities (fine/firm) to reach the Penguins. A World Record can be announced by the teacher.

4. Baton Bash: Divide the class into four groups by having each student in the class remove one shoe and place it in the middle of the gymnasium floor. The teacher tosses each shoe in one of four directions therefore forming four teams. Each student gets a relay baton or Lummi stick and a Frisbee. A square around one basketball court (up to half court) is set up (see diagram). Team #1, team #2, team #3, team #4 face,

inward on the half basketball court up along the sidelines and place their baton or Lummi stick in front of themselves.

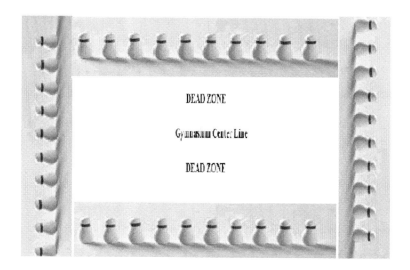

On the teacher's command, "Go!" everyone throws their Frisbee at the other team's batons and attempts to knock them down. When one team has at least one baton standing that team is declared the winning team.

Rules: All throws must be below the waist and lightly throw for accuracy not power. The center area is the Dead Zone. Players can retrieve a Frisbee from the Dead Zone but must throw from behind the batons. If a baton is blocked by a student, i.e., foot guard, the baton is automatically knocked over as a penalty and the person gets a 30 second penalty.

Safety: Slide the Frisbees along the floor. Keep your head up. Slow/low velocity throws only. This game can become slightly treacherous so the teacher must control it closely.

5. **Game**: 2 Square: Two large areas with four pylons (a square) are set up (see diagram).

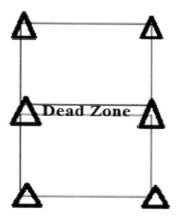

One team stands inside one square facing a team in another square with the Dead Zone in the middle. Everyone on the team is numbered, i.e., 1-15. Number one player throws into the square of the other team. If anyone on the team catches it, no points are awarded. If the Frisbee is dropped the throwing team gets a point. play continues up to 10 points. After throwing, the next numbered player (#1, 2, 3, etc.) throws next. All throws must enter the other teams square below the waist level or below the top of the pylons.

Strategy: Let the Frisbee fly out the back or the sides of the square area without touching it which results in a lost turn by the throwing team.

Culminating Activity/Game

6. Ultimate Frisbee: Outdoors is preferred. Use the four teams from Frisbowl and add two groups together to form two large teams. Two pylons are set up at each end of the field or gymnasium which is the touchdown area (see

diagram). One team starts with the Frisbee. The objective is to cross the Frisbee across the other team's goal line.

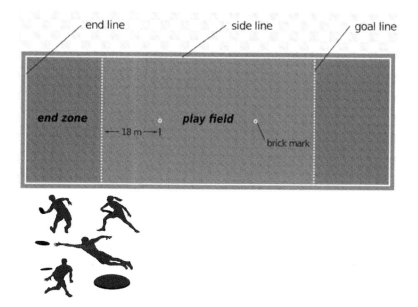

Rules: A player with the Frisbee can take three steps or hold the Frisbee for three seconds. A player must not pass the Frisbee back to the teammate he/she received it from (no give and go plays). If the Frisbee goes out of bounds, the other team brings the Frisbee in where it went out. A team must pass the Frisbee in for a touchdown and cannot run it across the touchdown line. When a team intercepts the Frisbee that team plays on with the Frisbee in their possession. If a player knocks the Frisbee down, the defending team who knocked it down takes the Frisbee and begins play. Play continues until five touchdowns in which a winner is declared.

NOTE: The new sport Disc Golf is a good activity to incorporate with Lesson #14. The way to teach Disc Golf can be found on https://www.pheamerica.org.

Lesson #14

Skill: Throwing

Theme: Space Awareness

Sub-Theme: High, Medium, Low

Equipment: Variety of balls

Teaching Tips: Safety discussion, refresh teaching the throwing technique

Warm Up

1. Toss and catch the ball to a partner throwing high and low.

2. Jog and pass and catch to a partner high and low.

Skill Development

3. Get a partner and practice baseball pitching. Switch every five pitches.

4. With a partner, throw and make over the shoulder catches.

5. Wall Baseball: Find a partner to compete against. Divide the playing area by using pylons (see diagram).

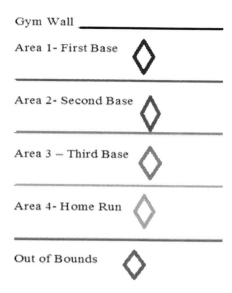

Gym Wall

Area 1- First Base

Area 2- Second Base

Area 3 – Third Base

Area 4- Home Run

Out of Bounds

Play begins by one person throwing a ball off the wall. The opponent tries to catch it. If it is dropped in a section, the thrower scores that base. For example, if the catcher is standing is in Area #1 (Single Base) and drops it, the thrower gets a single. If the catcher catches three balls off the wall that equals three outs and the thrower is changed. Play continues for three innings. The player with the most runs wins.

6. Partners can become a team and play another pair in a Wall Baseball competition. Two versus two.

Culminating Activity/Game

7. There and Back Baseball (throwing version): This game can be played using the skill of throwing or striking. A home base is set up as in a regular baseball game. First base is set up behind what is usually the pitcher's mound (see diagram).

100

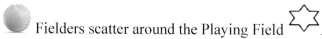 Fielders scatter around the Playing Field ☆.

The class can play either a Throwing game or Striking game. In the throwing game, no t- ball stand is used. In the Striking game, a t-ball stand is used. The ball used is first a whiffle ball (slow) then a gas ball (faster) then tennis ball (very fast). In either the throwing or striking game, the class is divided into two teams (one group at each corner of the gymnasium). Everyone on one team receives a number, i.e., #1-15. Player #1 on a team starts at bat while the 14 other players are fielders, Player #2 on the batting team is catcher. No pitcher is used. #1 hitting player throws the ball out to the field (if playing throwing version). After the throw anywhere to the outfield, he/she runs to the pitcher's mound base and back again. If the fielders throw the ball back to the catcher before the hitter makes it to the one base and back to home plate he/she is out. If #1 makes it the base and back one run is scored and the #1 hitter stays at bat. After the #1 hitter is out, #2 hitter goes up and #3 comes in as catcher.

NOTE: If the hitter makes it to the base and back he/she stays up and hits (or throws) again. The player accumulates as many runs as possible before being out.

Rule: The player cannot stop on the one base. If the throw or strike beats the hitter back to home plate he/she is out. There is no tag out as you are only trying to beat the throw back to home plate. The hitter is out if the ball crosses home plate before the runner.

NOTE- It does not matter if the catcher drops the ball or catches when the hitter is coming home. A run is determined by the ball timing arriving at home plate before (an out) or after (run scored) the hitter gets there. A World Record for runs for one player in one inning is announced to the class by the teacher, i.e., 20 runs. Two games are playing at once at the two diagonal corners of the gymnasium (back to back). The fielders are given the opportunity to field in either game.

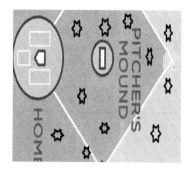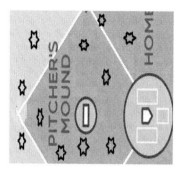

Games are played back to back diagonal across the Gymnasium

The game continues until all 15 students on one side of the gymnasium get a chance to bat (throw or strike). The winning player is the students with the highest accumulated runs after three innings.

Lesson #15- Special Day Activity- Archery

Skill: Teamwork, Listening, Safety

Equipment: Bows and arrows, targets with scoreboard on it (1 to 10 points), score sheet and clipboard, arrow quivers, rope,

Teaching Tips: Safety discussion on retrieving arrows, crossing the safety line, bringing out the arrows before class, teach stringing and unstringing the bows (stepping through), teach shooting technique (elbow high, two fingers on the tip, straight arm, guide feather towards the shooter), teach pulling arrows out from ground and pulling arrows out of the target after shooting (thumb and forefinger around the arrow-V shape).

Teams: Divide the class into five groups and each group lines up behind a quiver (with three arrows in the quiver) and one target.

Skill Development

1. Straddle the Line. Feet on either side of the safety line (rope).

2. Pick up your first arrow (Reach behind into the quiver and pick up an arrow).

3. Knock your arrow to the ground (Point the arrow while in the bow to the ground).

4. Aim. At this point, the teacher looks around to see the area is secure to shoot.

5. Anchor (Pull arrow back fully).

6. Release gently/fire at will.

7. Repeat. Pick up your second arrow. Continue the above commands and continue for all arrows.

8. After all Arrows are shot teacher says, "Put down your bows."

9. Retrieve your arrows and count your score.

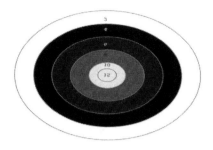

10. Report your score to the teacher.

After reporting the score, the second shooter goes up. One round is when all students from each group have shot.

NOTE: If there is an odd number in one group, the teacher can choose one student to shoot twice for that group. If there is a shortage of targets, two students from different groups can be standing on either side of the quiver shooting at the same target. This maximizes participation but students have to keep track of which three arrows are their shots. An Archery Winner Team Award is given to all members of the winning team after so many rounds.

Modification: Students bring in old posters they no longer want to shoot at. More arrows per round are provided.

Lesson #16

Skill: Striking

Theme: Effort Qualities

Sub-Theme: Fine and Firm

Equipment: Striking implements (plastic paddle racquets, tennis racquets, baseball bats - plastic, wood, aluminum, squash racquets, racquetball racquets), variety of small balls (tennis, gas, whiffle), pylons, poly spots

Teaching Tips: Safety discussion on swinging a racquet, teach striking technique (wrist action, transfer of weight, building torque (recoil), follow through), hand-eye coordination discussion, coincidental timing discussion, task complexity discussion.

Warm Up

1. Discussion. Task complexity spectrum for the skill of striking (easy to most difficult factors effecting striking). Show class all striking implements and rank from easiest to most difficult. Use the three criteria for ranking implements on task complexity. 1) Weight of the implement, 2) Length away from the hand the implement is, 3) Size of the striking surface of the implement.

2. Students take one implement based on their hand-eye coordination ability, i.e., if you have great hand-eye coordination take a baseball bat (which is the most difficult to strike with). Everyone gets a ball. Strike the object into the air lightly with your implement.

3. Next strike the object into the air hard and high (up to but not hitting the ceiling) with your implement.

4. Next use non-dominant hand for both light and hard strikes with your implement.

Skill Development

5. Chose a partner. Use one ball only to toss five pitches to the partner who is close (10 feet) and he/she will strike the ball back. Then switch. Work on accuracy in striking back to the partner.

6. Toss five pitches to the partner who is farther away (30 feet) and the partner strikes the ball back with accuracy. Switch.

Culminating Activity/Game

7. Hot Pursuit: Divide into groups of six. One person with a racquet is chased by the other five other members who have one ball. The teammates pass the ball to each other and attempt to throw the ball at the person holding the racquet. The person holding the racquet protects themselves by striking the ball away with the racquet. The person who keeps the racquet the longest, wins. The student who has the racquet the most times is also a winner. Discuss safety in throwing below waist and the philosophy about the use of people as human targets (throw light objects - throwing for accuracy not to hit someone).

8. There and Back Baseball (striking version): See rules and set up in **Lesson #14 Culminating Activity**. Can also be played when throwing is the skill focus instead of striking. A home base and a first base at or behind the traditional pitcher's mound are used. In the striking version of the game a t- ball stand is used (created from a golf tube stuffed into the top of a pylon works great). The class can play either a throwing game or striking game. In the throwing game, no t-ball stand is used. In the striking game, a t-ball stand is used. The ball used is first a whiffle ball (slow) then a gas ball (faster) then a tennis ball (very fast) in either the throwing or striking game. The class is divided into two teams. Everyone on one team receives a number and stays at one end of the gymnasium. For example, numbers #1-15. #1 player on a team starts at bat while the 14 players on the other team are fielders. #2 player on the batting team is catcher. No pitcher is used. #1 hitting player strikes the ball out to the field (if playing striking version). After the strike anywhere to the outfield, he/she runs to the pitcher's mound base and back

again. If the fielders throw the ball back to the catcher before the hitter makes it to the one base and back to home plate he/she is out. If #1 makes it the base and back one run is scored. After the #1 hitter is out, #2 hitter goes up and #3 comes in as catcher.

NOTE: If the hitter makes it to the base and back, he/she stays up and hits (or throws) again. The player accumulates as many runs as possible before being out.

Rule: The player cannot stop on the one base. If the throw or strike beats the hitter back to home plate he/she is out. There is no tag out, as you are only trying to beat the throw back to home plate. The hitter is out if the ball crosses home plate before the runner.

NOTE- It does not matter if the catcher drops the ball or catches when the hitter is coming home. A run is scored by the ball arriving at home plate before the hitter gets there. A 'world record' of runs for one player across one inning is announced to the class by the teacher, i.e., 20 runs. Two games are playing at once at the two diagonal corners of the gymnasium (played back to back). The fielders are given the opportunity to field in either game (see diagram).

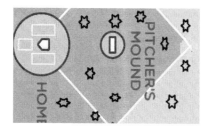 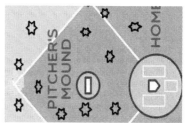

Games are played back to back diagonal across the Gymnasium

The game continues until all 15 students on each team get to go up to bat. The winning player is the player with the highest accumulated runs after so many innings.

Lesson #17

Skill: Dribbling

Theme: Effort Qualities

Sub-Theme: Fast and Slow

Equipment: Variety of large balls (soccer, playground), pylons, poly spots

Teaching Tips: Safety discussion. Keeping the soccer ball below waist when shooting or passing, coincidental timing discussion.

Warm Up

1. Jog slowly around the gymnasium using all the space. On the whistle, jog fast into an open space and stop. Teach open space principle.

2. Everyone get a soccer ball. Dribble slow with the soccer ball. On the whistle, stop your ball and sprint to another ball and continue dribbling it.

3. Stretch. Form a circle of six. Dribble over to a classmate. They will stop the ball and form a stretch. Continue until everyone shows two stretches.

Skill Development

4. Demonstrate and teach dribbling technique.

5. Have the students dribble slowly with the ball and on the whistle speed up and on next whistle slow down.

6. Dribble slowly and when you come to a green (or name a color) gymnasium floor line, turn quickly and sprint two steps with the ball. Then dribble slow again.

7. Choose a partner. Dribble up to the partner and slowly dribble around the partner and then dribble back to where you started. Pass to the partner and the partner takes a turn.

8. Next, same as above but begin with passive defense, which means the defense does not try to take the ball away but forces the partner to work on dribble around a defender.

9. Same as above but partner goes to active defense which means using some minor effort to try and take the ball away while the partner goes around the partner.

10. Shuttle drill. Three students facing three students. Dribble and pass.

XXX   XXX

11. Divide into groups of five to six students and form a circle. Dribble in and out around the circle and call a classmate's name. Pass to that person and he/she will dribble in and out through entire circle and call a name and pass.

12. Same as above. Number each group member #1-6. Teacher calls number. Everyone with that number dribbles in and out of the circle. The first one back in all groups wins a point for their group.

Culminating Activity/Game

13. Woodpecker: Reinforce safety in kicking. With pylons, form a large circle around the gymnasium with the whole class inside the circle area.

The whole class will dribble inside a circle area marked off with pylons. All students dribble inside the pylons and when the teacher calls "Go!," the students attempt to peck (kick) another player's ball out of the circle while maintaining a dribble with their own ball.

Rules: If your ball is kicked outside the circle, you must go directly out and cannot attack another player's ball while you are leaving. Once you are out, you become a Judge standing outside the circle of the pylons. Judges watch as balls roll out of the playing area and determine if they cross the pylon before a save was made, like a line judge in tennis.

Modification. Use two circles of pylons and when a student is out in one circle you go to the other circle and continue playing there.

14. 4 Goal Soccer: Form four teams with different color pinnies/markers. Set up four soccer nets. A player can score in any of the other three nets while defending their own. Keep score amongst your team. The team with most goals wins the Soccer Championship Award.

Modification: Four goals and only two teams instead of four teams. The activity creates a cognitive challenge (going to one goal straight ahead and then switching direction to go to another goal). You can also add a second ball.

Lesson #18 - Special Day Activities - Unit Ending Activities - Around the World

Skill: Hopping, Running, Scooting, Crab Walk, Jumping. Gallop

Equipment: Pylons, one scooter board, music CD with travel songs, country passport, country posters, marker, stamp for stamping the passport

Teaching Tips: Safety discussion

Warm Up and Skill Development

Shuttle Run: Three to three. First person runs across gymnasium and tags second person across the gymnasium. Second person runs to third person and so on. Complete all six rounds running, then do a side shuffle, then backwards running, etc.

Culminating Activity/Tournament

Six Stations are sectioned off in the gymnasium and divide the class into six groups. The activities focus on skills, teamwork and students learn about countries (Geography). One appropriate travel-related song is played for the duration while groups are at each station. Station set up of the pylons is exactly the same for all six stations. Only the movement differs (easy equipment set up). See diagram below which is set up for all 6 stations.

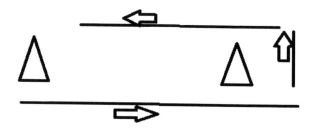

Station 1 - Australia (poster on the wall of the country)

Students start behind a pylon and hops to a pylon across the gymnasium (20 feet) one student at a time. The first student hops on one foot (Like a kangaroo) to the pylon across the gymnasium, goes around it and comes back again (change hopping legs to other leg to complete last half) and tags the next person in line. Continue until the song ends. See how many students can complete the Australia task in the allotted time.

Station #2 - USA (poster on the wall of the country)

Students start behind a pylon and runs to a pylon across the gymnasium (50 feet) one student at a time. The first student runs (Like a road runner) to the pylon across the gymnasium, goes around it and comes back again (change to running backwards to complete last half) and tags the next person in line. Continue until the song ends. See how many students can complete the USA task in the allotted time.

Station #3 - Canada (poster on the wall of the country)

Students start behind a pylon and crabwalk to a pylon across the gymnasium (10 feet) one student at a time. The first student crab walk to the pylon across the gymnasium, goes around it and comes back again and tags the next person in line. Continue until the song ends. See how many students can complete the Canada task in the allotted time.

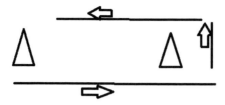

Station #4 - Antarctica (poster on the wall of the country)

Students start behind a pylon and scoots by scooter to a pylon across the gymnasium (20 feet) one student at a time. The first student scoots on the scooter board (scoots like a penguin does when on their belly) to the pylon across the gymnasium, goes around it and scoots back again and tags the next person in line. Continue until the song ends. See how many students can complete the Antarctica task in the allotted time.

Station #5 - England (poster on the wall of the country)

Students start behind a pylon and leap frogs to a pylon across the gymnasium (20 feet) one student at a time. The first student leap frogs over five teammates. (Leap frog was invented in England in late 1800's.) to the pylon across the gymnasium, goes around it and runs back again and tags the next person in line. After the first student is leap frogged over, he/she should line up to be tagged next, the others prepare in a leap frog position. Continue until the song ends. See how many students can complete the England task in the allotted time.

Station #6 - Mexico (poster on the wall of the country)

Students start behind a pylon and gallops to a pylon across the gymnasium (10 feet) one student at a time. The first student gallops (Like a horse) to the pylon across the gymnasium, goes around it and gallops back again and tags the next person in line. Continue until the song ends. See how many students can complete the Mexico task in the allotted time.

PASSPORT

COUNTRY	NUMBER OF CHECKMARKS
AUSTRALIA	
USA	

CANADA	
ANTARCTICA	
ENGLAND	
MEXICO	
TOTAL	

Lesson #19 - Special Day Activities - Unit Ending Activities - Pokémon (or change to another Current Day Cartoon)

Skill: Throwing, Hand Dribble, Striking, Catching, Overhand pass

Equipment: Create five stations with pylons (five areas of the gymnasium), two playground balls, six bean bags (two of each color), six cylinders (bowling pins), two scoops, 10 hula hoops, 15 pylons, three wooden or plastic paddles, one whiffle ball, 15 poly spots, Pokémon CD, scoreboard, magic markers, Pokémon posters, Pokémon energy cards (in abundance and easy to find in bundles)

Teaching Tips: Safety discussion

Warm Up and Skill Development

The teacher divides the class into five teams. Each student in the class picks a Pokémon card which is face down. There are five different Pokémon characters available on the cards (teacher can photocopy these images from the internet and place on index cards). Each student takes one card and looks at it to determine which team he/she is on. Five teams are created: Charizard, Dragonite, Sandshrew, Zapdos, Beedrill.

122

As the two minute Pokémon theme song plays, each team attempts to collect as many points as possible at each of the five stations around the gymnasium. The teacher may want to walk the class around to each station and perform one practice round with a chosen team to demonstrate. The teacher can verbally give instructions how the station is played (making reference to the poster board visually). Each team goes to one station and practice is given to each team for two minutes at each station prior to competition. Students use the poster board as a visual guide. During practice time, teams work on rotations and teamwork is used to devise speed strategies. The tournament is a cooperative event (within each team) and a competitive (between teams) tournament. Awards are given for the winning team. Participant awards are also given for all class members that tried his/her best. An authentic assessment is also given to the class in which each student has to take the self-evaluation home after completing it to have his/her parents sign and return it. The evaluation asks the student if he/she tried hard in class today or did not try as hard as he/she could have. Questions are also given on if the student worked as cooperatively as he/she could have (self-evaluation).

Culminating Activity/Game

Station #1. Skill: Hand Dribble. Dribble in and out of each pylon and run straight back after the after the half way point (see diagram). After running back, the student gives the ball to the next teammate. No dribble is required after the last pylon in the first row (the player runs straight back). Two points are scored for each complete run. If passed half way

point (end of the first row of pylons) when song ends, two
points are awarded.

STUDENTS HERE

XXX

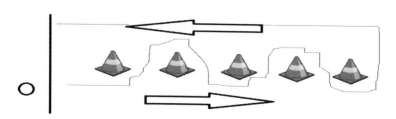

Station #2. Skill: Throwing: Each player throws six bean
bags at the six cylinders which are at three different
distances.

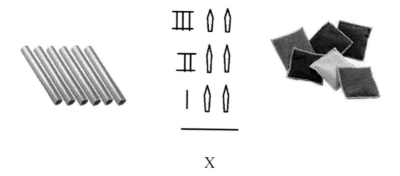

X

XXXX STUDENTS HERE

The closest two cylinders/batons score one point each for
being knocked over, the middle two cylinders are worth two
points each and the farthest cylinders are three points each.
Therefore, each player can score 12 points in total if he/she
hits all six cylinders with the six bean bags.

Rule: Cylinders are not set back up until all six bean bags are thrown. Each player throws at all six cylinders before a rotation of players occurs. Total score is for all teammates after the entire Pokémon song.

Station #3. Skill: Striking. One member of the group is designated as a pitcher. The pitcher then pitches a ball to a batter who has a wooden paddle.

The batter hits the ball to the outfield and one outfielder hits

the ball in the air before it lands on the ground to another

outfielder who also has a wooden paddle.

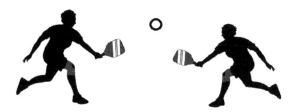

In other words, the outfielders keep the ball going in the air as long as possible between the two of them. The score is the highest consecutive points total by two players on one team (how many times they kept the ball off the ground). Once the ball hits the ground everyone rotates and new outfielders receive the ball. Play continues for the two-minute song and only the one highest score counts for the team score.

Station #4. Skill: Passing. Students stand in a big circle of 6 team members designated by poly spots. The first student passes the ball to the second student and so on clockwise around the circle. After all passes are made and the ball returns to the first player, he/she puts the ball down and runs to the next player's spot. Players all move to the next clockwise spot to stand and wait. The last player who moves to the original spot picks up the ball and begins passing around the circle. One point is given for each full rotation back to the start. If the ball is halfway around when the song ends the team scores one point.

Station #5. Skill: Catching. Two players stand with scoops and one of the scoops has a ball in it. A third player holds a hula hoop at shoulder height.

The player with the scoop and ball tosses the ball to the other player attempting to get it through the hula hoop held by the third player. If the ball goes through the hoop and is caught one point is awarded. If the ball does not go through the hoop but is caught it is zero points but play continues. If the ball drops to the ground the three players rotate and three new players from the sideline take over. The score is the highest consecutive points earned by two players without the ball hitting the ground. Only one score, the highest score, is recorded for the team after the two-minute song ends.

Tournament Results - End of the Class

Teams reconvene after completing all five stations and a Pokémon Championship Team is awarded a Pokémon Championship Certificate. As the class comes in for the awards, all equipment is picked up and brought in by each team at the last station they completed. As a bonus, the teacher offers Pokémon Energy cards for special students who worked hard. The teacher can say the added boost cards can help the students go into writing exams.

Teaching Tip: Students can bring in their own Pokémon memorabilia to put up on the walls or around the gymnasium and the teacher can have the students in Art class design posters and decorations for the stations.

Lesson #20 - Special Day Activity - Fitness Monopoly 2

Skill: Fitness

Equipment: Strength/fitness bands, three step stairs, 10 pylons, Monopoly money, stop watches

Teaching Tips: Safety discussion on fitness activity.

Principles of cardiovascular muscular strength, heart rate and flexibility principles are taught to students and then these concepts will be applied at stations set up in the gymnasium. The activities focus on teaching health related concepts at the same time that students complete a physical education activity.

Read: Vamos, S. and Sawicki, T. M. (2003).

Divide the class into five teams. Teams collect as much Monopoly money as possible through individuals on the team. The teacher makes stations labelled GO, Free Parking and Holding Pen. Everyone meets at GO and receives $200. Have teams leave from GO and start at one of the five stations.

GO - $200

Station #1: Tennessee Avenue **Bicep** Curls

Easy - 20 repetitions with blue band

Medium - 20 repetitions with purple band

Hard - 20 repetitions with red band

Station #2: St. Charles **Abdominal** Crunches

Easy - Lay on back and lift shoulder for two seconds - 20 repetitions

Medium - Feet on floor and knees bend 45 degrees - 20 repetitions

Hard - Legs in air and knees at 90 degrees - 20 repetitions

FREE PARKING $200: Stop here for five minutes and receive $200 (use stopwatch)

Station #3: Virginia Avenue **Push Ups**

Easy - Knees and feet on ground – just arms- 20 repetitions

Medium - Knees and feet on ground – arm first then rest of body- 20 repetitions

Hard - Basic push up - body off the ground at all times- 20 repetitions

HOLDING PEN: Penalty area for teacher determined lack of effort for two minutes - $100 penalty (use stopwatch)

Station #4: Baltic Avenue **Running**

Easy - Shuttle Run- pylon and back 20 feet - 20 repetitions

Medium - Shuttle Run- pylon and back 30 feet - 20 repetitions

Hard - Shuttle Run- pylon and back 40 feet - 20 repetitions

Station #5: Mediterranean Avenue **Step Ups**

Easy - One Step- Step Up - 20 repetitions

Medium - Two Step - Step Up - 20 repetitions

Hard - Three Step - Step Up - 20 repetitions

Object of the Tournament

Individual students collect as much Monopoly money as possible and hand it in for a team total. Start to GO, collect $200 and then move to one of five stations. Chose a level: Easy, Medium, or Hard. If the student makes the 20 repetitions at the chosen level, he/she receives Monopoly money equated to that level. $100 for Easy level, $200 for Medium level, $300 for Hard level. Not reaching the 20 repetitions at the chosen level results in zero money for you and your team. Any students not providing their best effort, the teacher sends him/her to the holding pen for a two-minute penalty and forfeits $100. After all students have completed the five stations and collected money for their accomplishments, all teams meet at GO and tally their total money. A Fitness Monopoly Award is given to the team(s) with the most money collected (May also want a Gold, Bronze, Silver, Participant awards).

Chapter Three

Conclusion

The approach a teacher uses to teach physical education is critical to the lasting impression students will take way from the experience. Teachers should plan for student success and ensure the experience is safe and enjoyable for the students. By creating a safe and enjoyable experience in physical education the students are more likely to want to continue physical education and physical activity for the rest of their life. Putting competition in perspective for the students through the movement education approach that has been demonstrated in this book will allow for a positive physical education experience. The teacher should always emphasize to students that winning or losing is not as important as doing the best they can.

There are several strategies a teacher can take to reducing the competitiveness of the class. Playing non-competitive games is one way. There is an abundance of cooperative games that emphasize aspects of games other than competition, such as emphasizing good sportsmanship and teamwork. Modifying traditional activities to reduce the competitive factor is another way. Implementing things like all touch rules and all score rules will enhance cooperation and reduce competition (Sawicki, 2000).

A final consideration is not to play activities which use people (students) as human targets, or that have elimination as a specific feature of the activity. Teachers should avoid games which eliminate students. These games often have the same students eliminated first, leaving those students feeling inferior which in turn creates a lack of enjoyment for those students in the class. Games like dodge ball use human targets and are elimination games. During play, players are given permission by the teacher (through the games rules themselves) to throw a ball at a fellow classmate. Proponents against dodge ball believe this creates a situation of distrust between the students and the teacher because the teacher is allowing and actually encouraging a form of violence against the students. Some teachers who are against dodge ball-type activities believe the ball is an extension of the fist. Further, dodge ball uses terms like "murder ball", "death ball", and "jail" as part of the game jargon. The detrimental aspects of games that use people as human targets far outweighs the few outcomes the students will take away from the activity (Williams, 1992).

If physical education is to promote healthy, safe and enjoyable experiences for the students, then the teacher must closely consider the games he/she is playing. Many students will readily endorse playing dodge ball, especially the more skilled ones. Ultimately, it is the teacher who decides what is best for the students in his/her physical education classes. Teachers have to remember the perception of physical education the students will come away with which can have a lasting effect on their participation in physical activity for years to come. In reality, most activities can be played and enjoyed by the entire class but the teacher has to use modifications to make sure the activities are developmentally appropriate (Sawicki, 2000).

Teachers have to work hard to plan lessons that are developmentally-appropriate, keep physical education standards in mind, and ensure every student is learning the skills and experiencing success in physical education class.

As physical education instructors teach the 20 lessons in this book, the teacher will slowly notice the emphasis on gaining points and providing awards for winning teams. I do this as a motivator but have found I can only do that because I change teams every day, pair strong athletes with weak ones, and emphasize continually that you may win one day, but the next day another team or other classmates will win and that is fine. Students really try hard for world records, and paper award certificates but also work hard simply for recognition that they succeeded in physical education class today. Rest assured, there is so much switching of teams, sometimes during the game on the spot, that every student in the class ends up winning both individually and as part of a team many times over during an academic year.

Many of these lessons develop skills outside the physical domain and this is the goal. It will be readily seen that social skills such as teamwork, cooperation, communication, empathy will be developed in the lessons. Emotional skills are also shown in the lessons such as personal behavior control, moral decision making, listening, positive reinforcement to others. Lessons take a multi-subject matter approach. This aids in cognitive development in areas such as math (addition), English (reading), geography, art, and music. Lessons should always be developed to enhance all aspects of the students holistically. Education through the physical is a means to gain so much more for each student in the class. The widest array of physical learning was demonstrated along with the holistic development of the social, emotional and cognitive aspects through this book, Teaching Students through a Movement Education Approach.

References

Creative Certificates. Retrieved from: https://www.creative certificates.com/physical-education-certificates/

Disc Golf. How to Implement Disc Golf Curriculum in Schools. Elementary School Heading. Pumnea, T. Retrieved from: https://www.pheamerica.org

Sawicki, T.M. (2000). Developmentally appropriate activities using games modifications, *Strategies,* 14(2), 22-29.

_____. (2002). Feed the Penguin: A game for developing skills. *Strategies,* 15 (4), 21-22.

Also at: https://docslide.com.br/download/link/feed-the-penguin-a-game-for-developing-skills

_____. (2005). First week activities for elementary and middle school teachers. *Teaching Elementary Physical Education* (TEPE), July, 8-9.

Also at: www.humankinetics.com/acucustom/sitename/Documents/DocumentItem/4894.pdf

_____. (2006). Line Basketball. http://www.teachingideas.co.uk/pe/linebasketball.htm

Vamos, S. and Sawicki, T.M. (2003). Fitness Monopoly for student and athletes. *Strategies,* 17, 17-19.

Williams, N. (1992). The physical education hall of shame. *Journal of Physical Education, Recreation and Dance,* 63 (6), 57-60.

About the Author

Dr. Timothy Sawicki (Ed.D, M.A., HB.PHED, B.Ed.) is currently the Director of the Online Physical Education Master's degree at Canisus College in Buffalo, NY. He has taught elementary physical education, high school physical education and college/university physical education for over 30 years. Dr. Sawicki has been teaching at Canisius College since the fall of 1997. He completed his undergraduate degree at Brock University, a Master's Degree at the University of Western Ontario and a Doctorate completed at the University of Toronto and University of Wisconsin. He is a certified K-12 physical education teacher. He is considered an expert in his field of motor development having written and presented at conferences on early motor development patterns in children. Dr. Sawicki founded the online physical education program at Canisius College and this program was the first fully online program at Canisius College (2006). The program has graduated over 600 graduate students from 32 different states and 10 countries. Dr. Sawicki's knowledge from his years of practice are enthusiastically shared in this book.

Email:

sawickit@canisius.edu

Linkedin:

http://www.linkedin.com/pub/dr-timothy-sawicki/60/246/9

Linkedin ONLINE PE:

https://www.linkedin.com/pub/canisius-college-onl-physical-education-masters-program/a5/1/48b